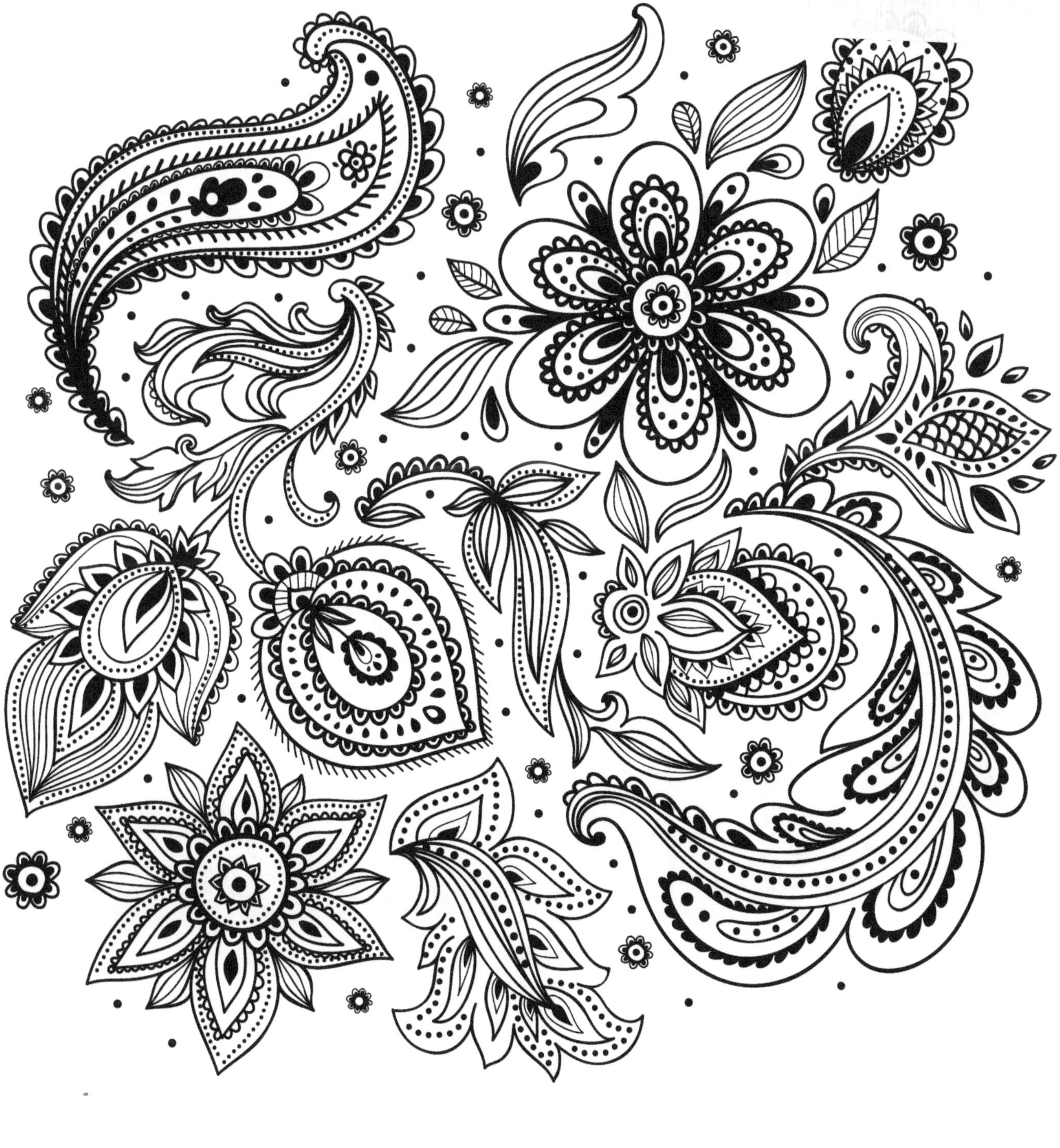

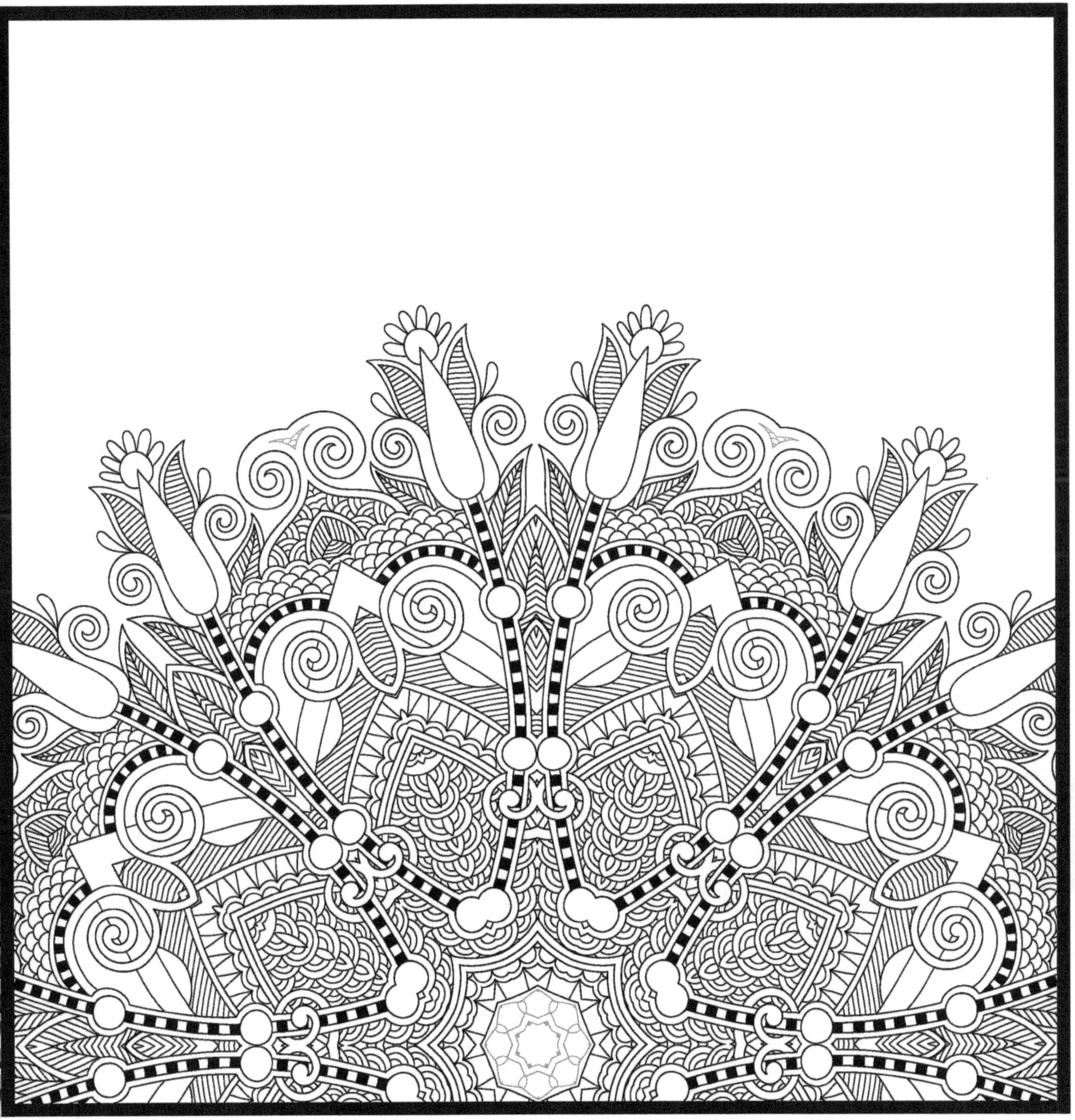

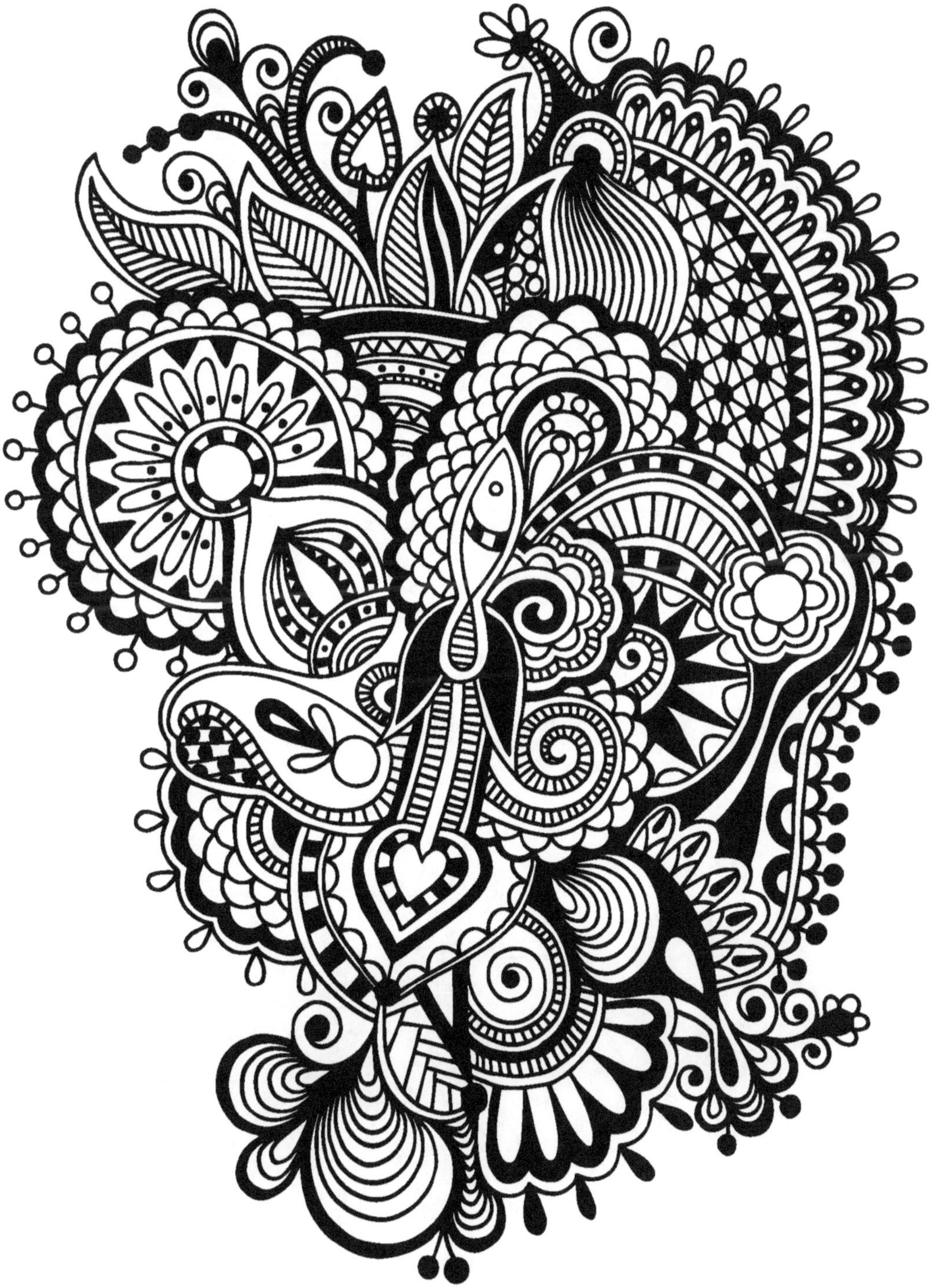

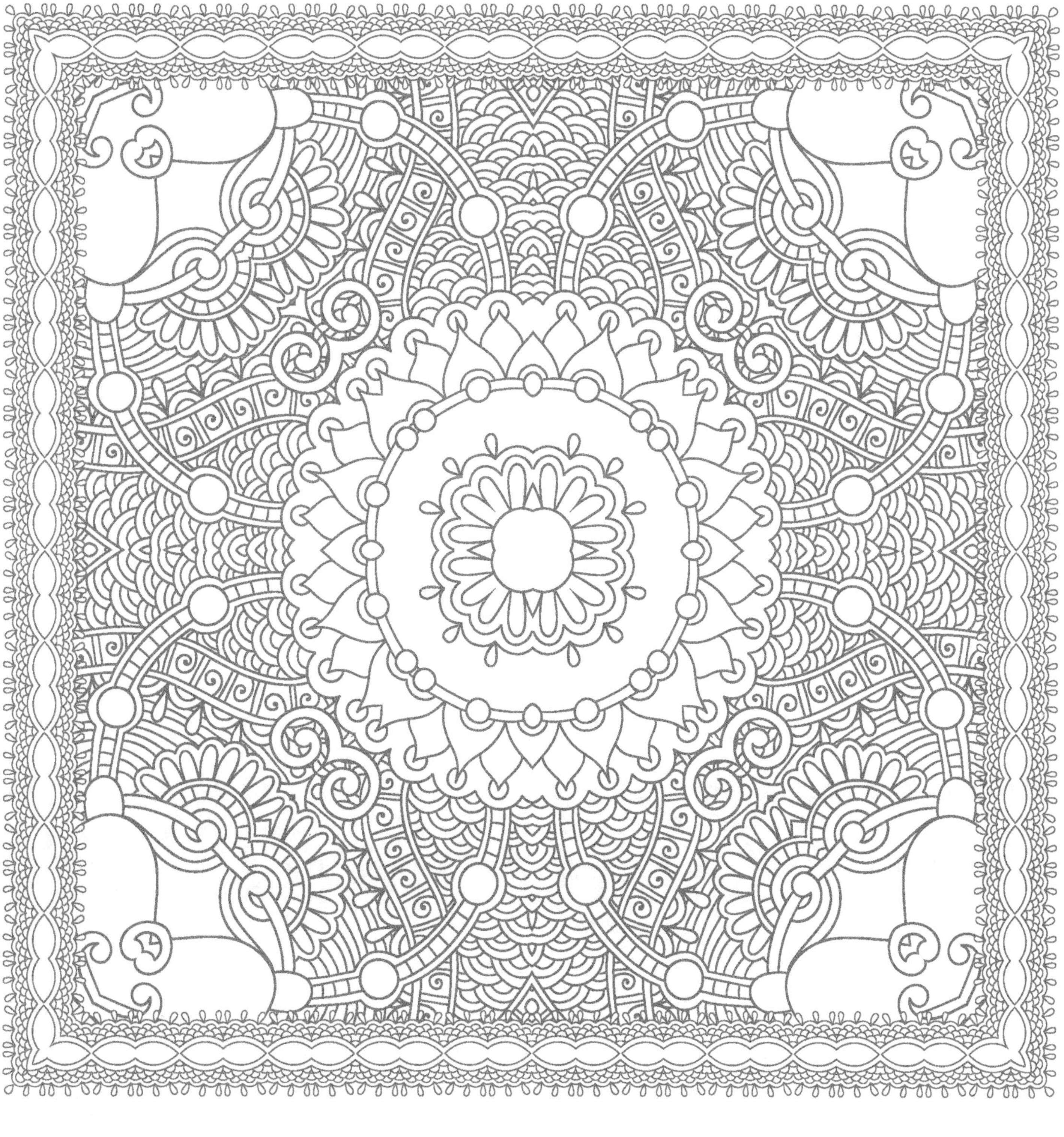

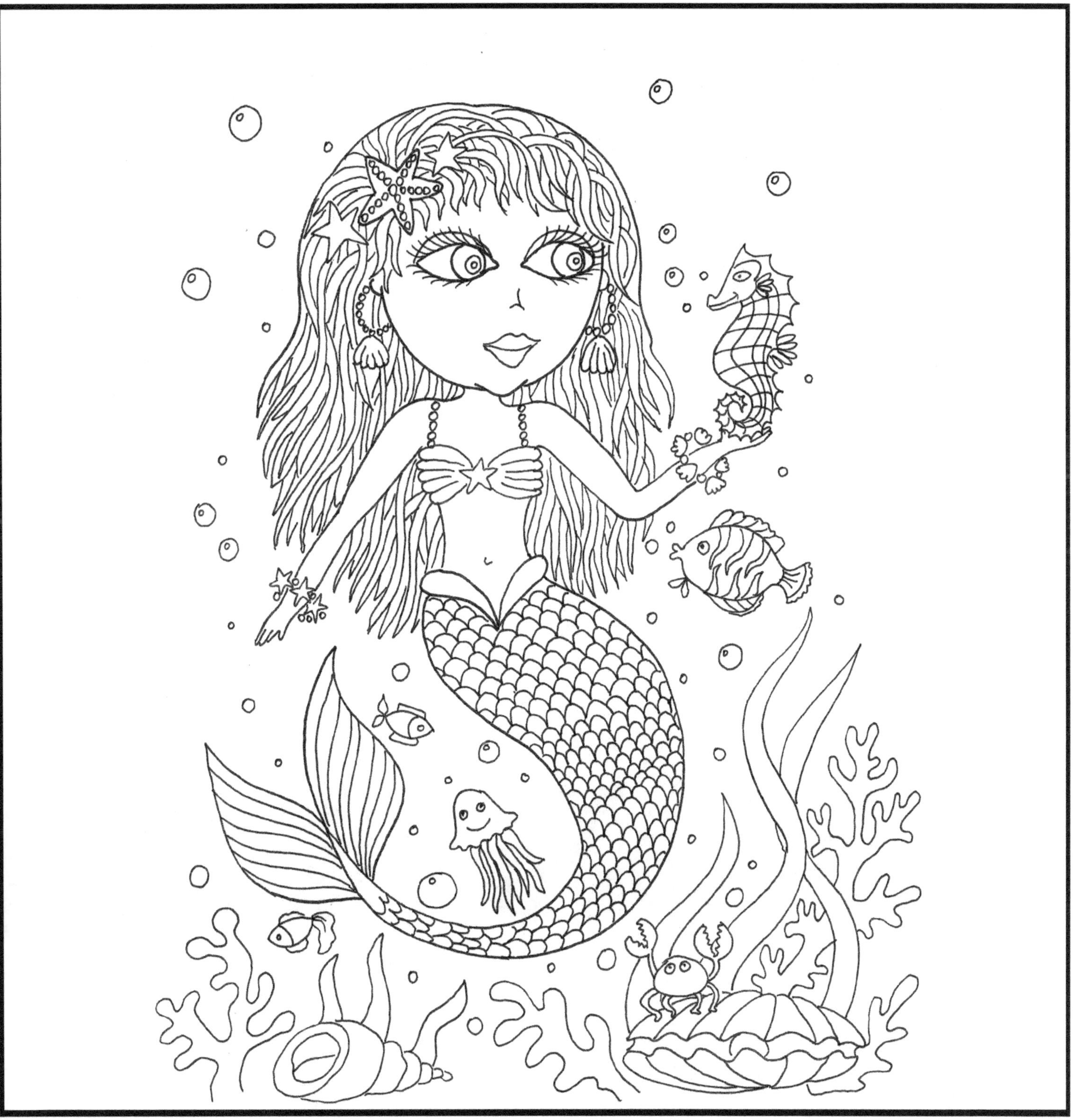

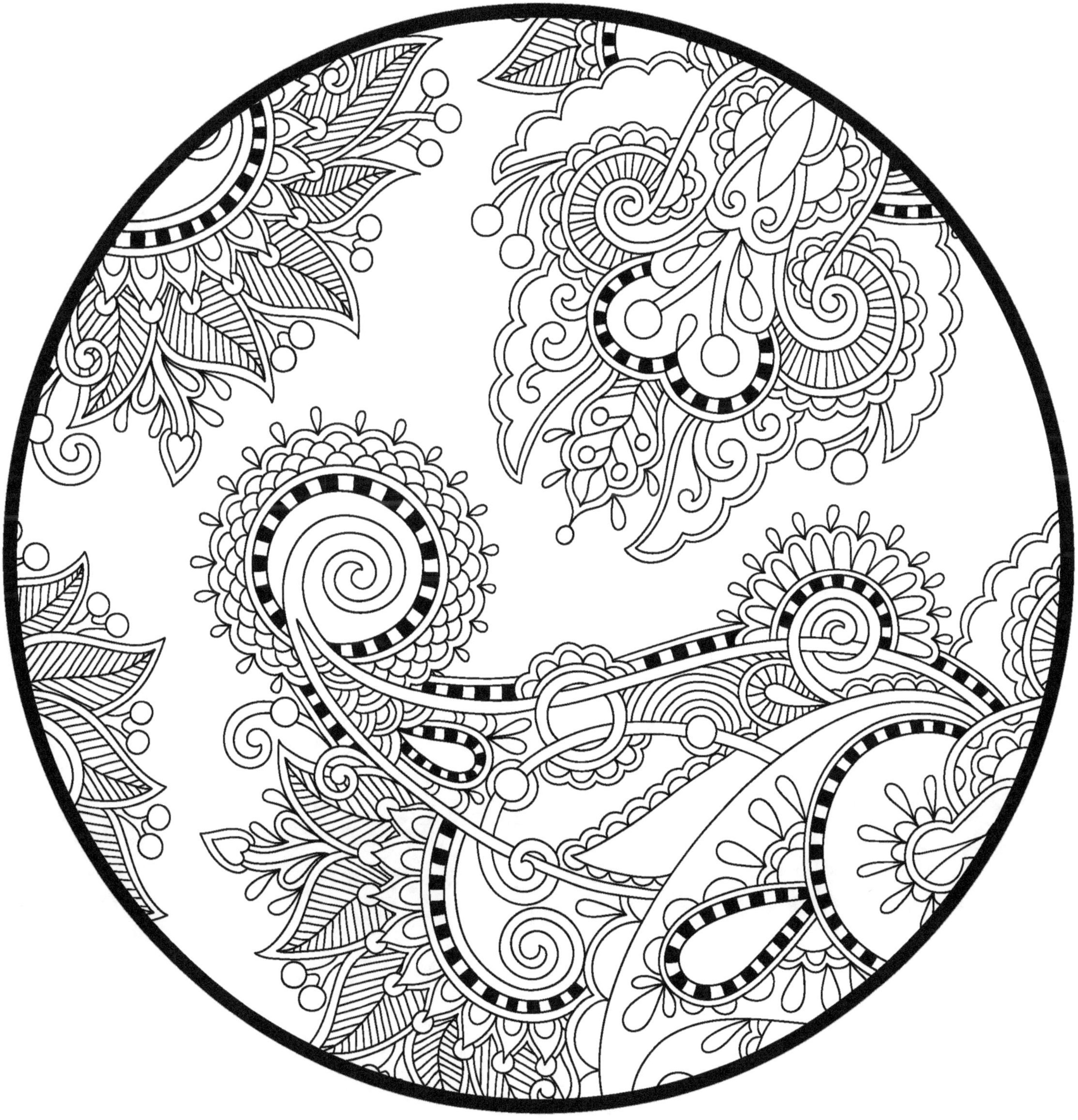

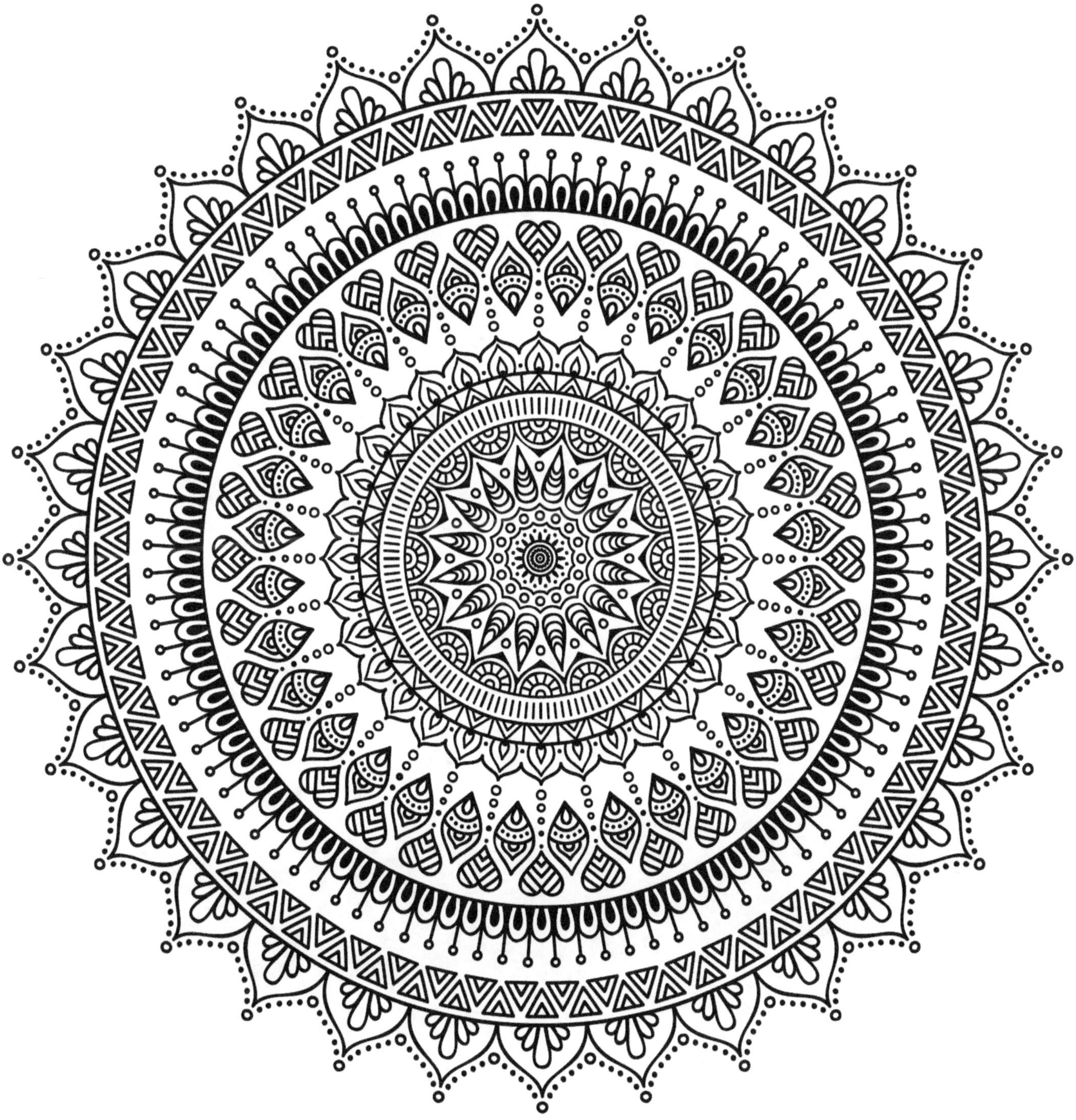

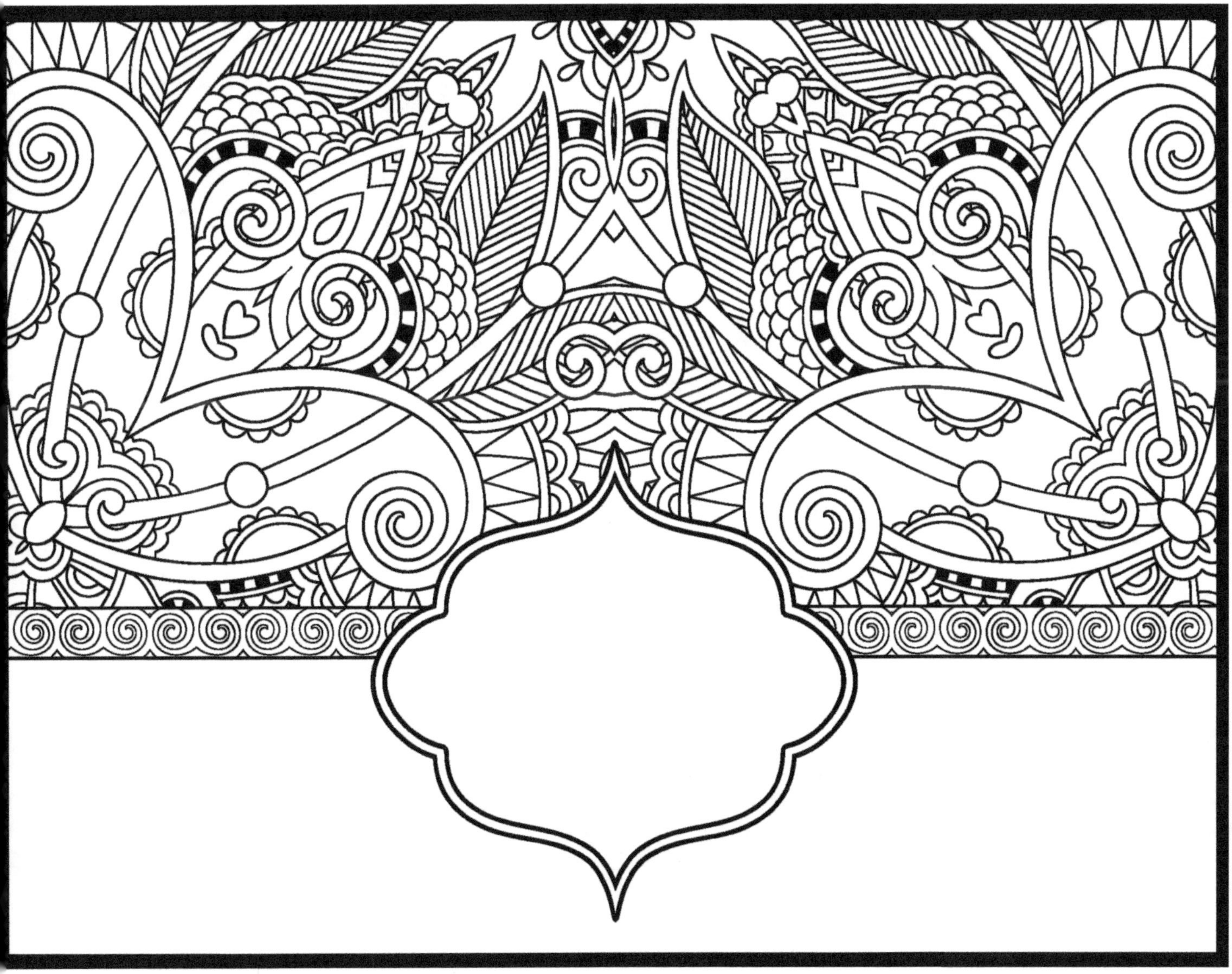

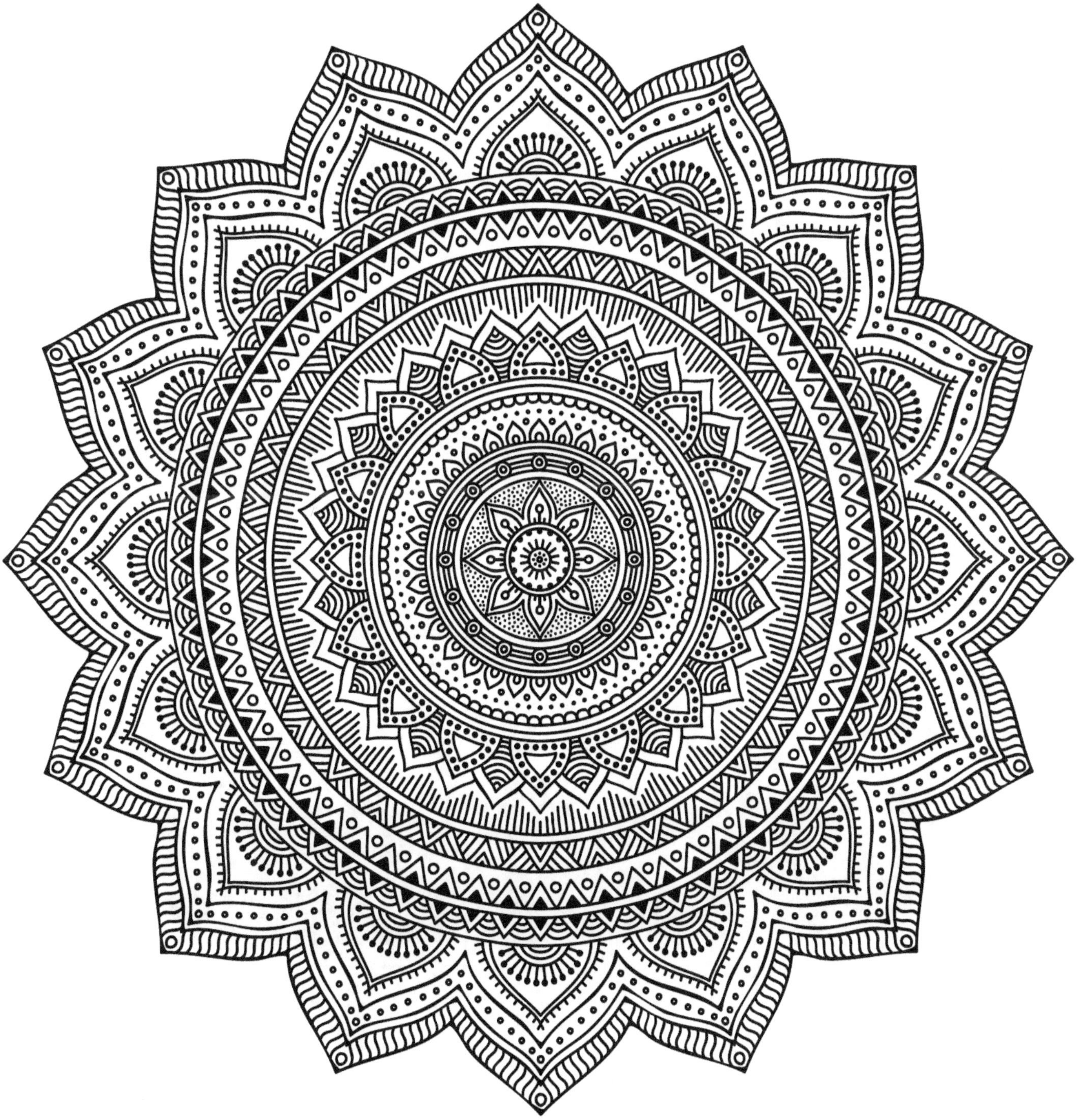

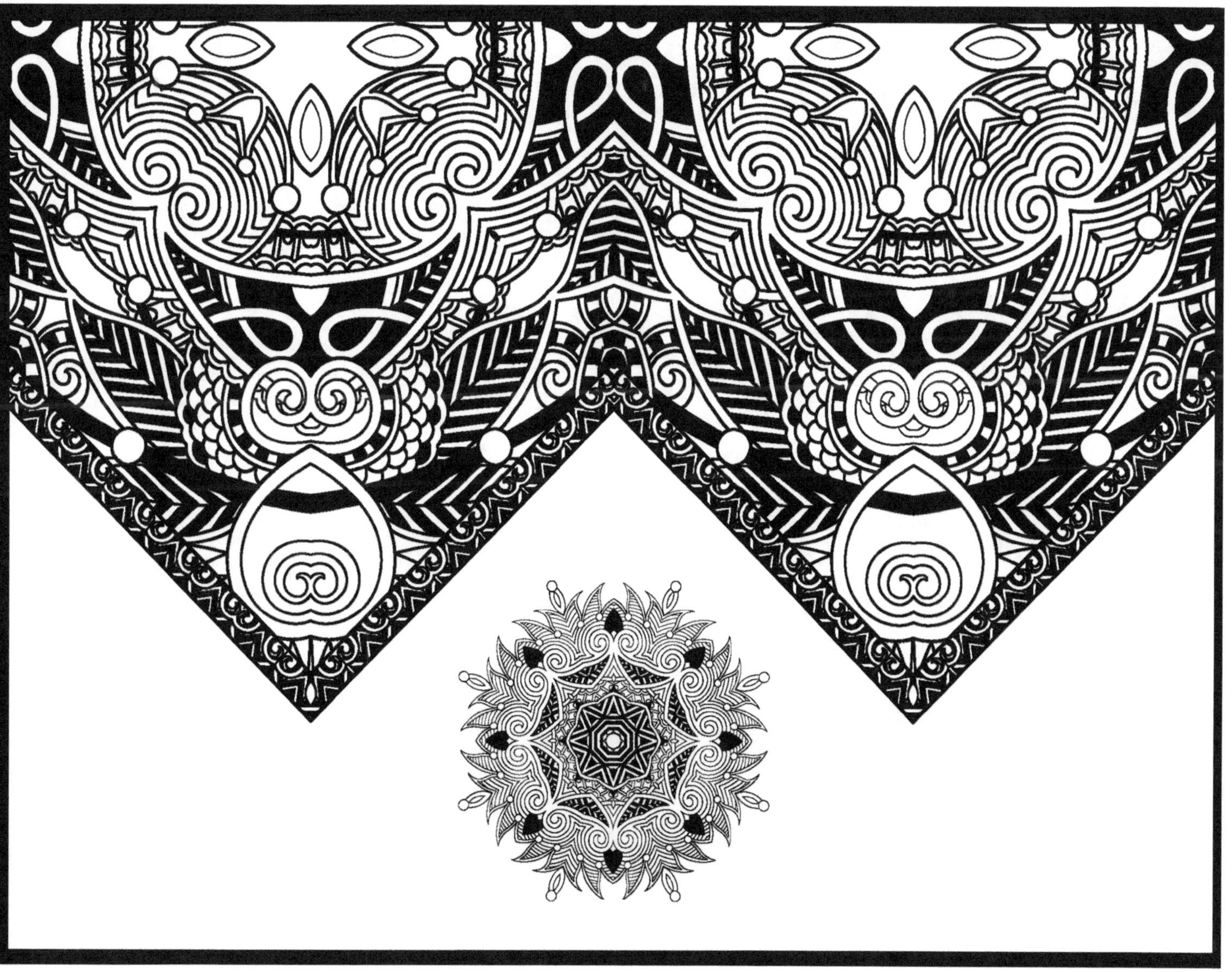

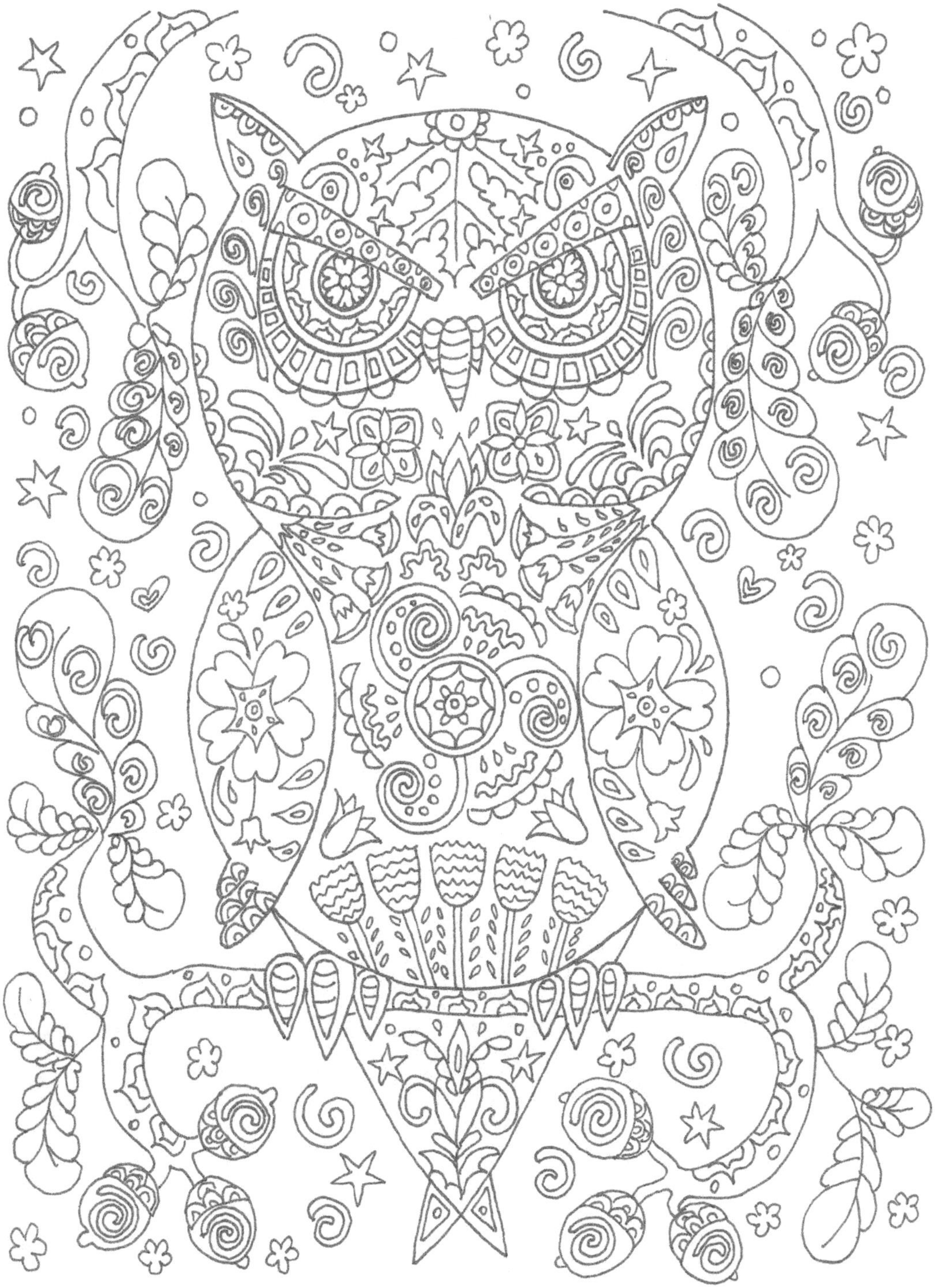

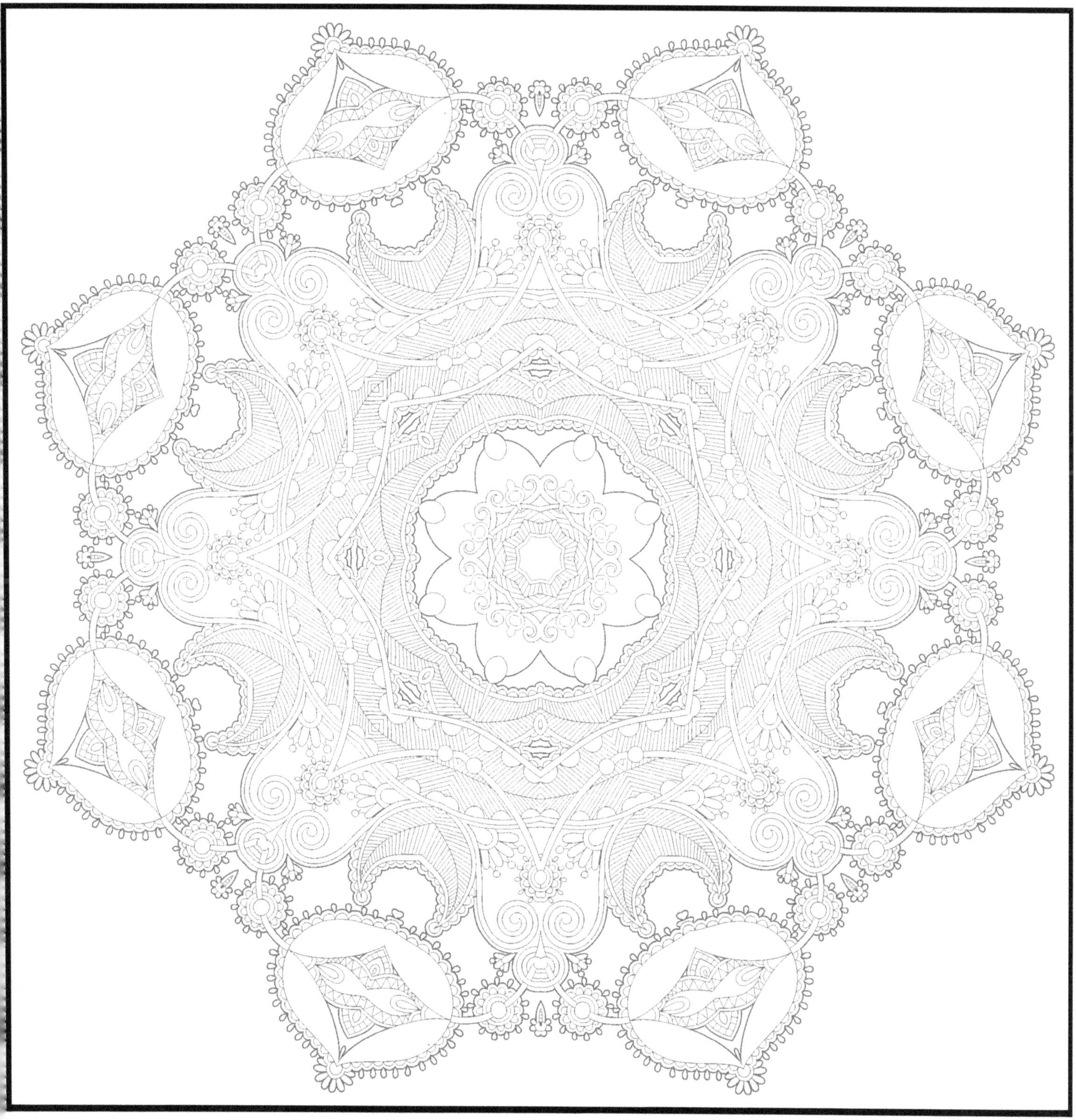

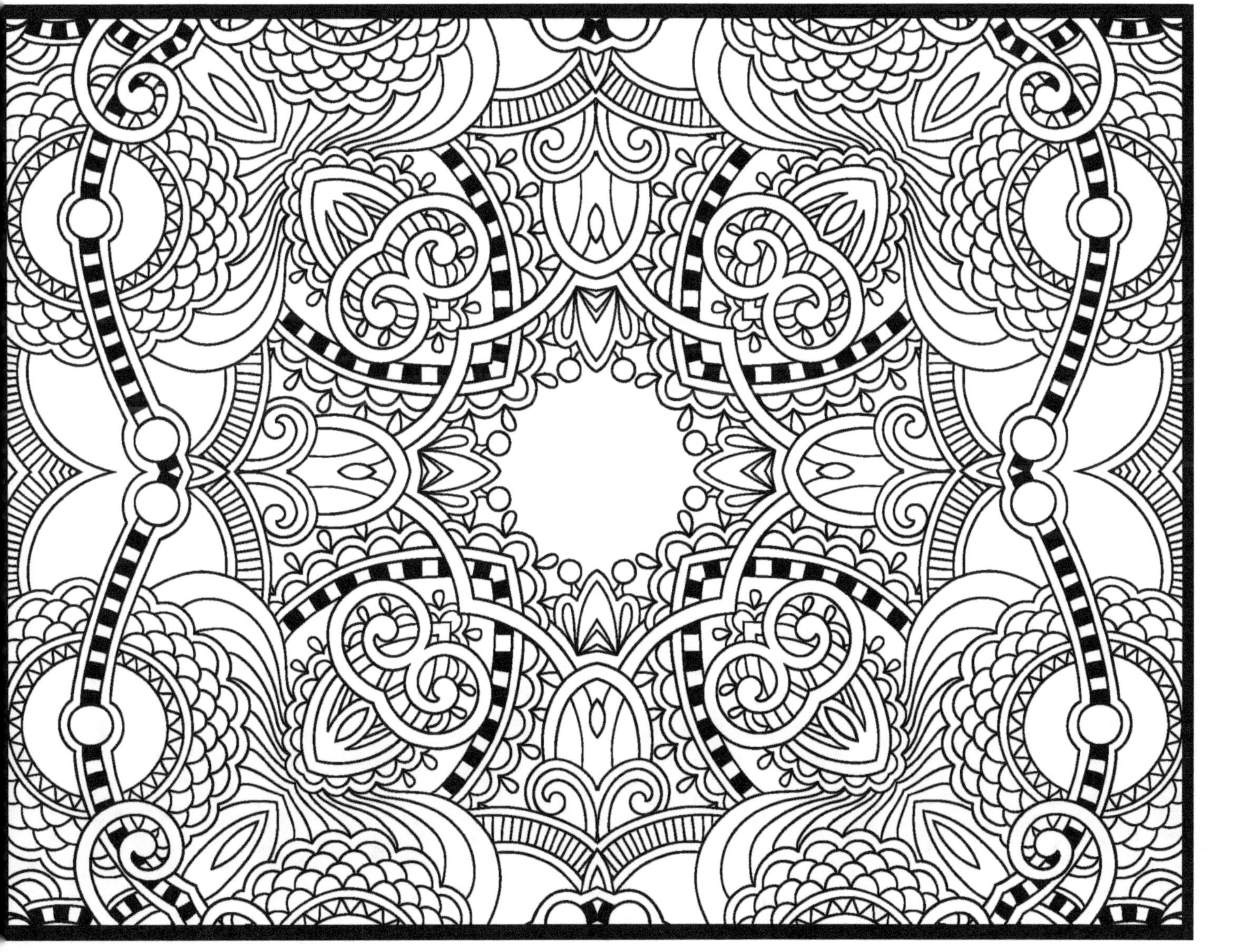

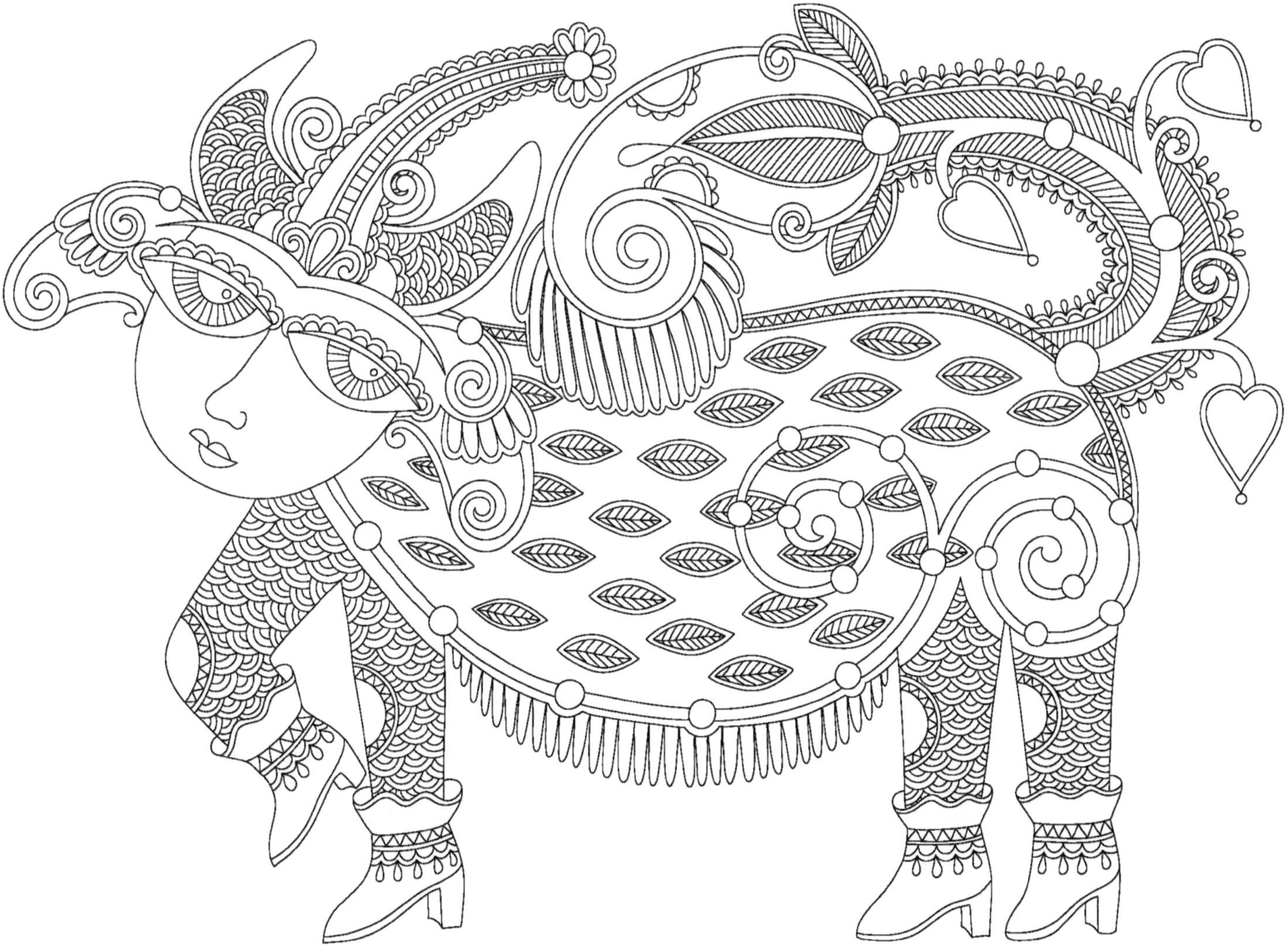

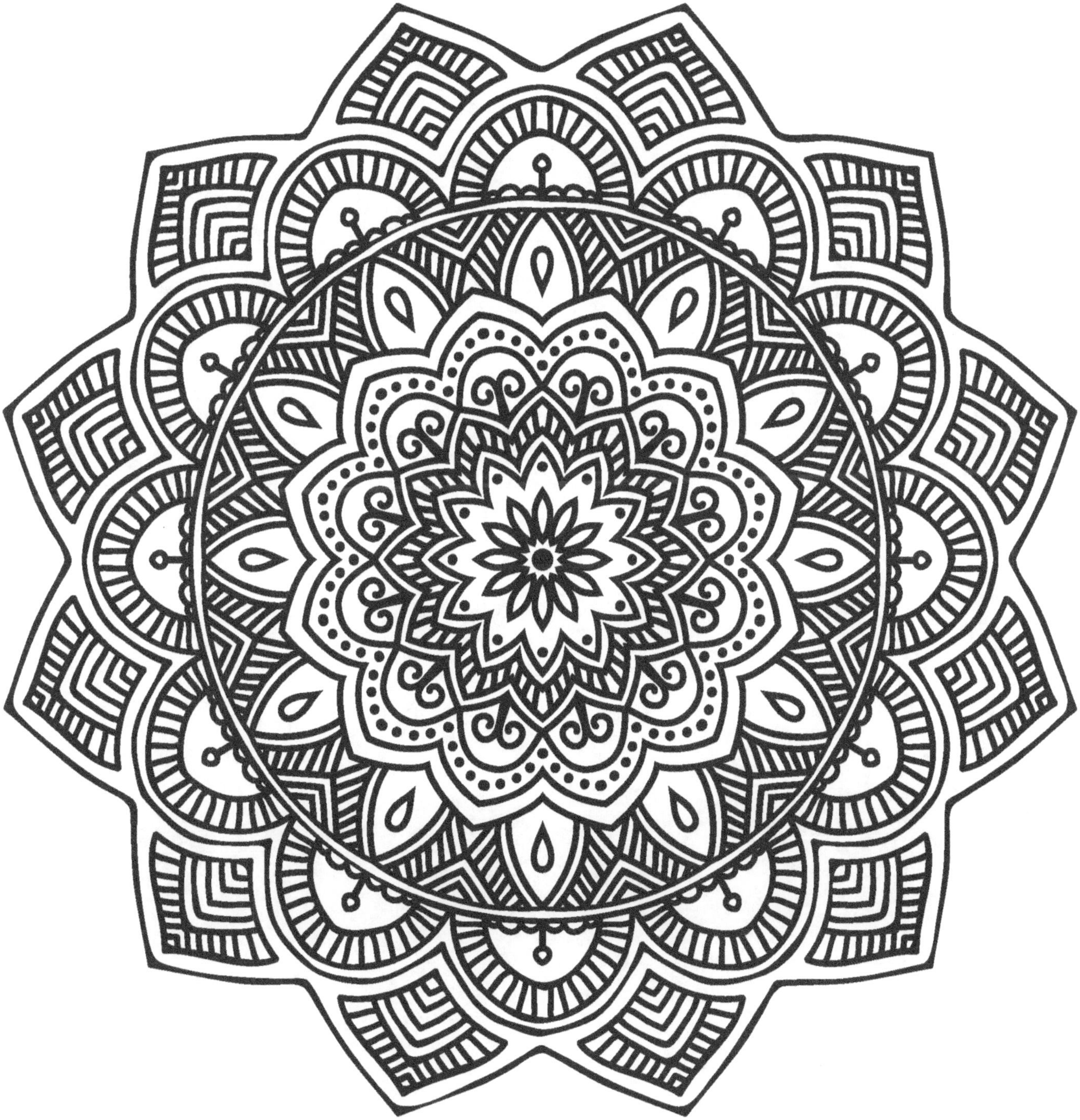

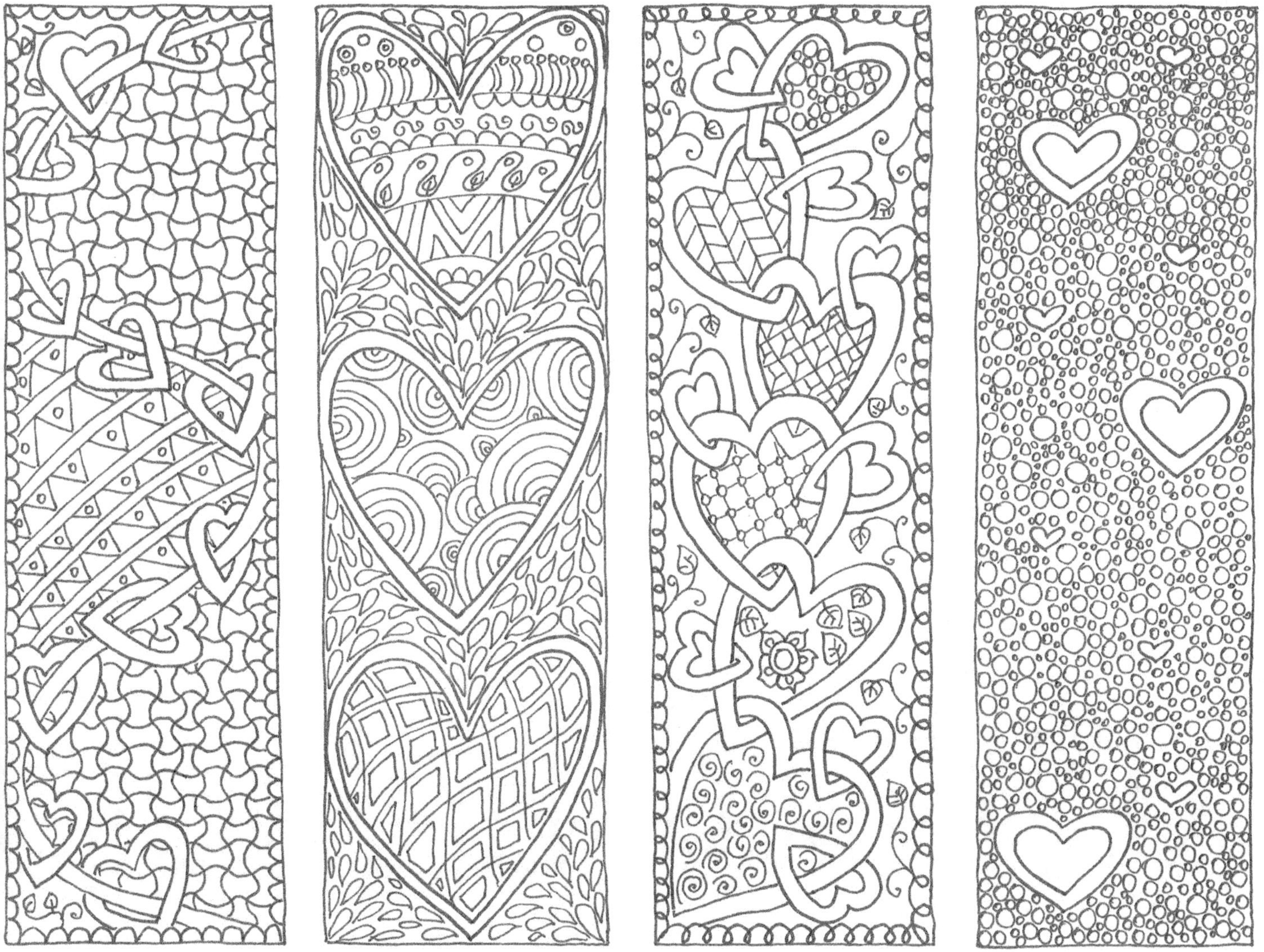

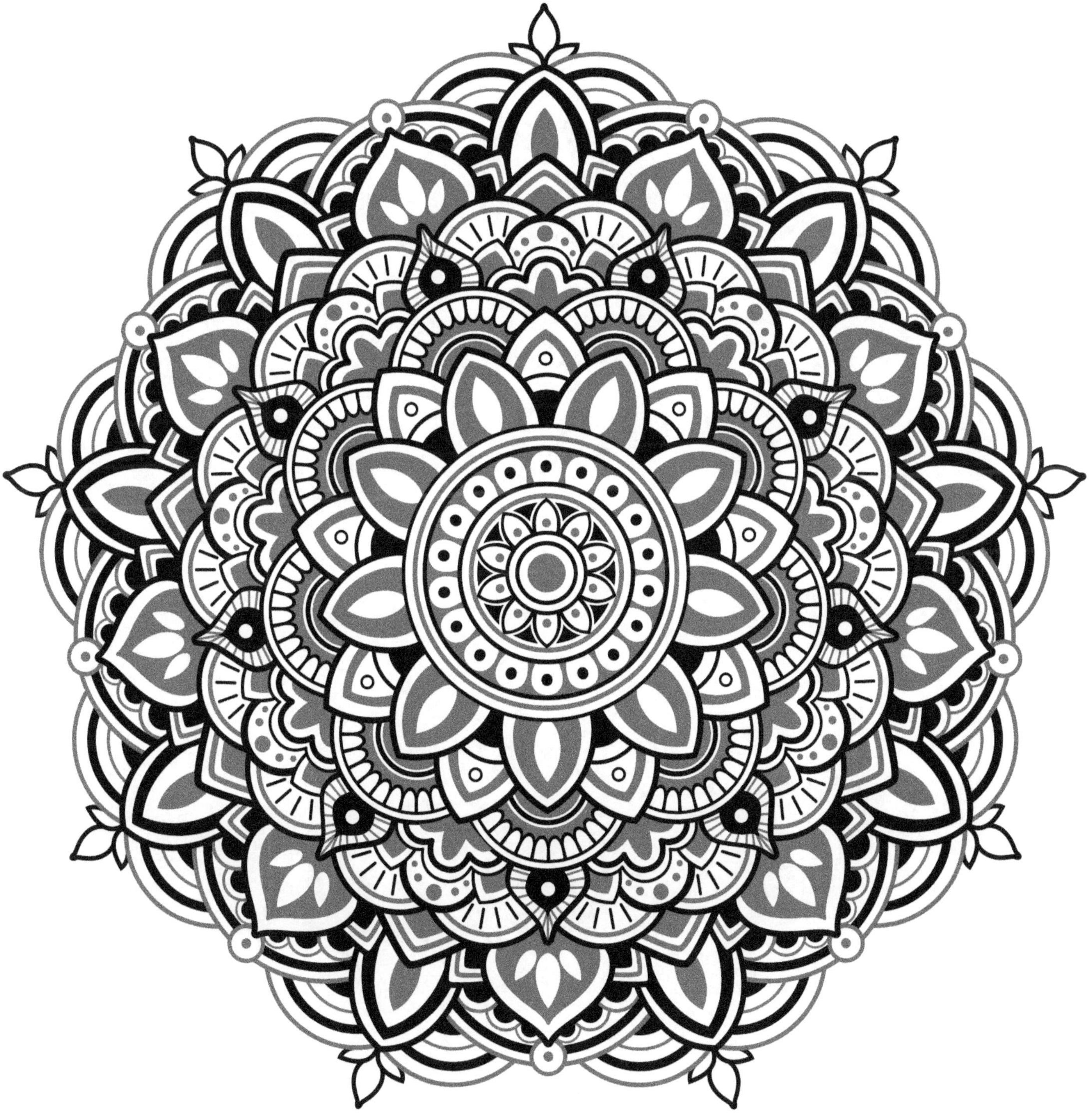

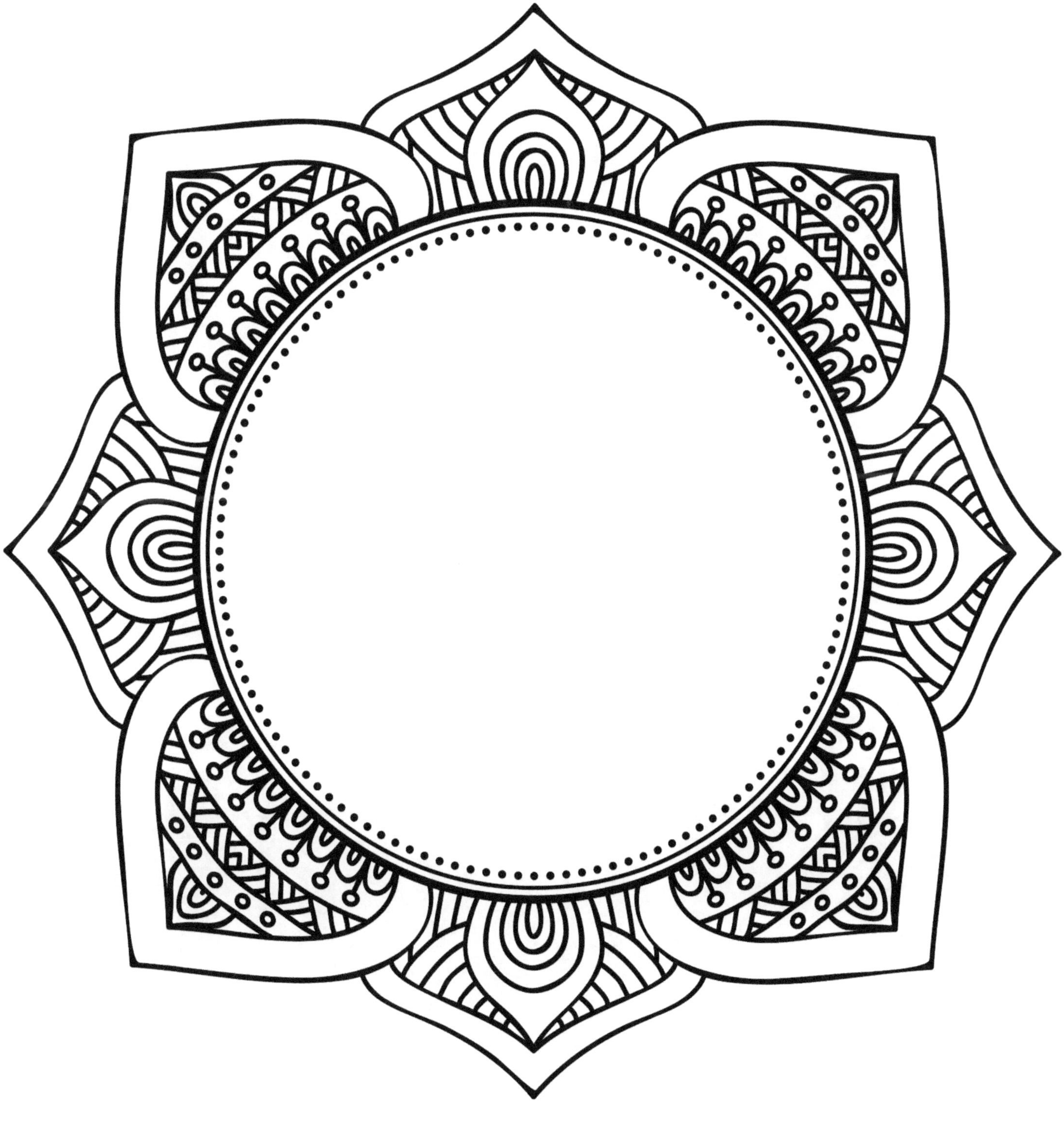

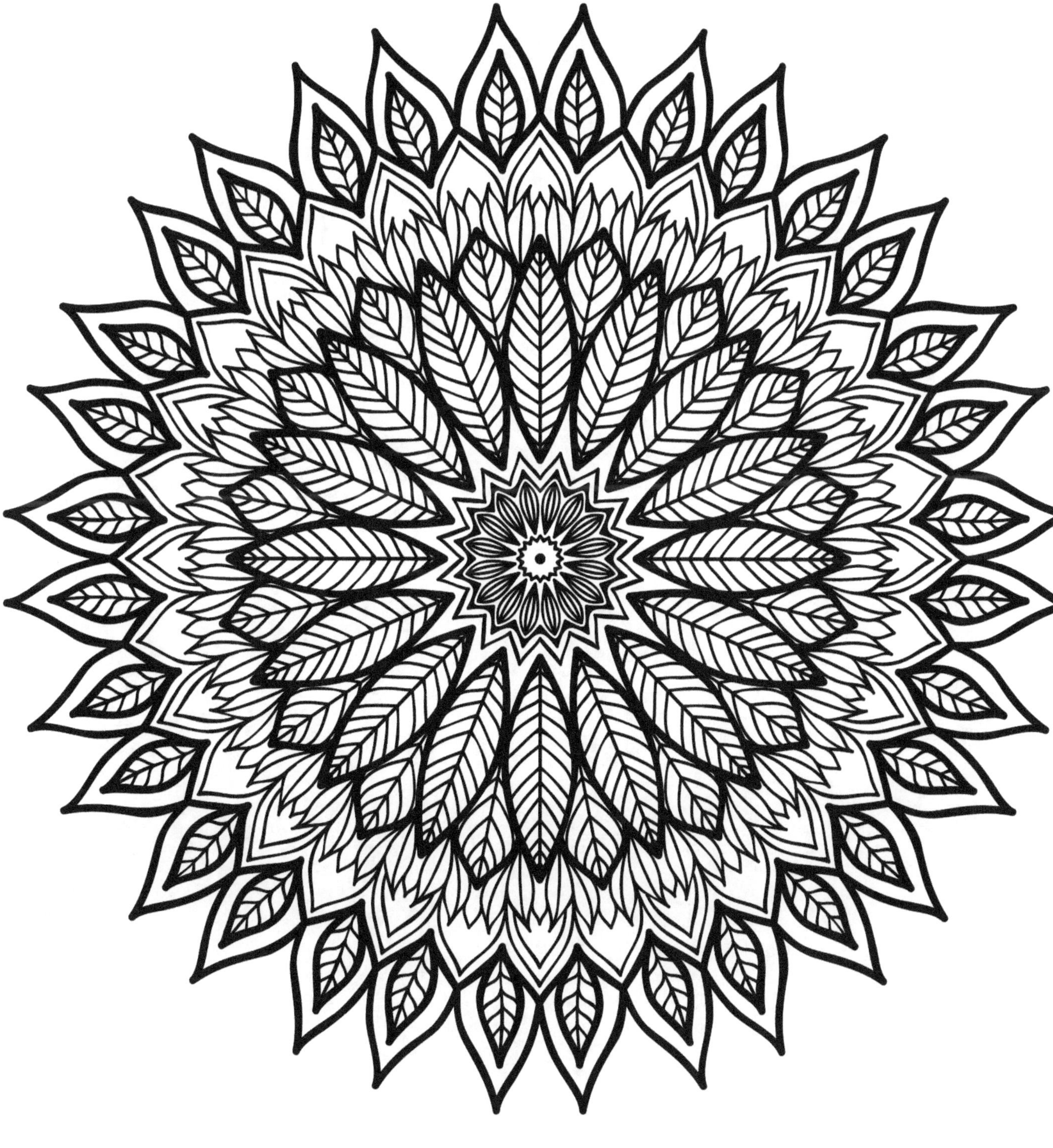

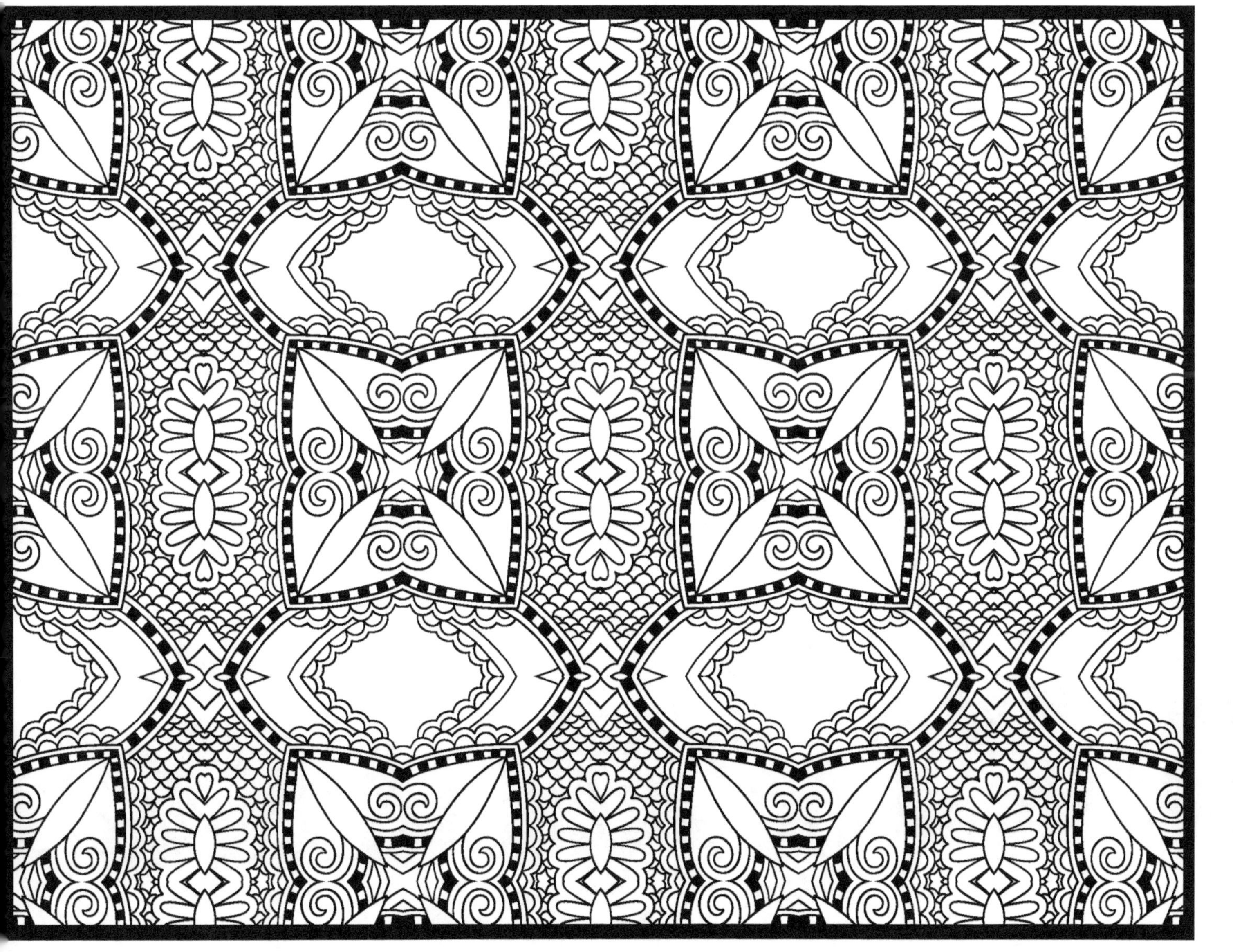

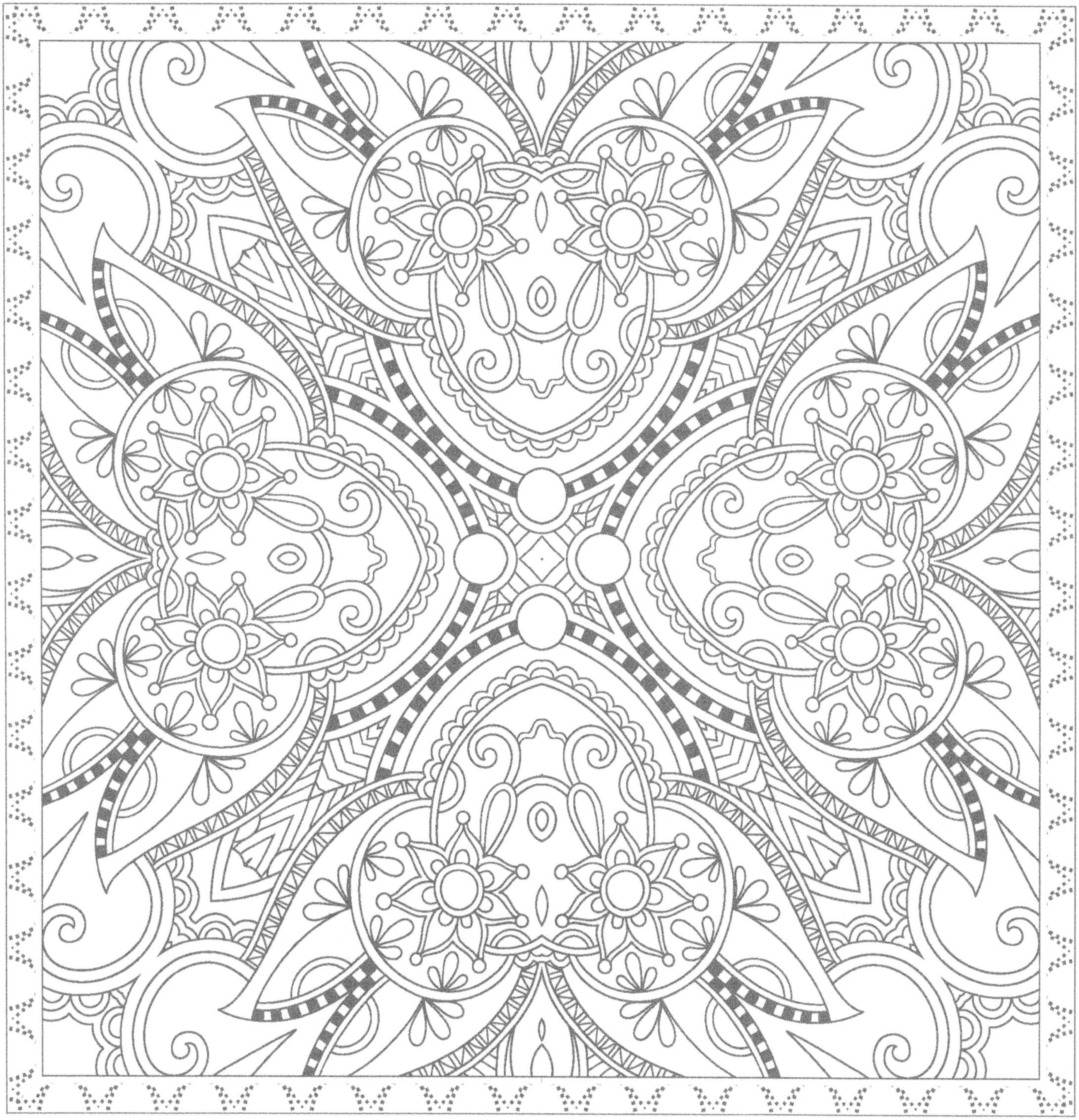

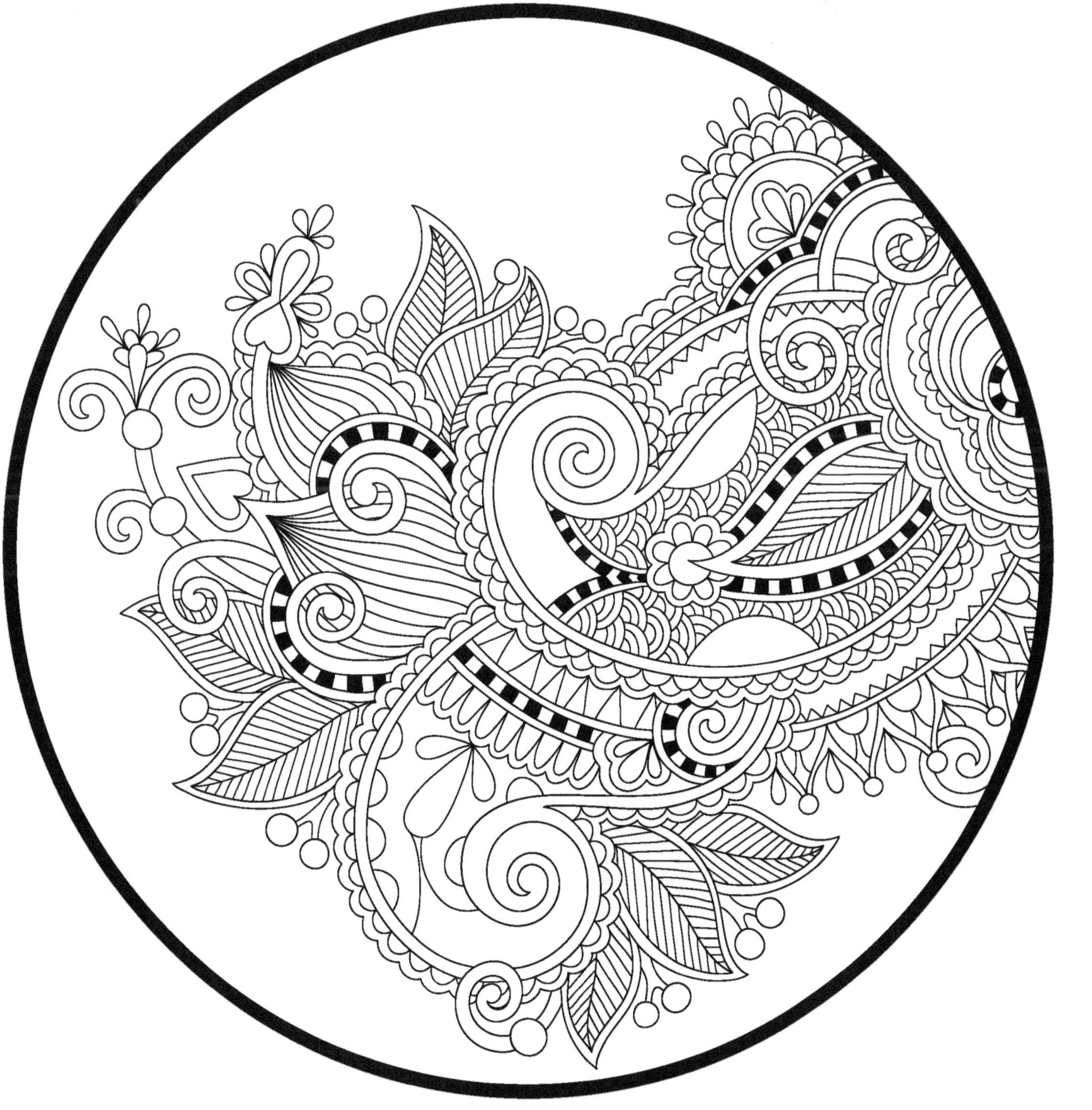

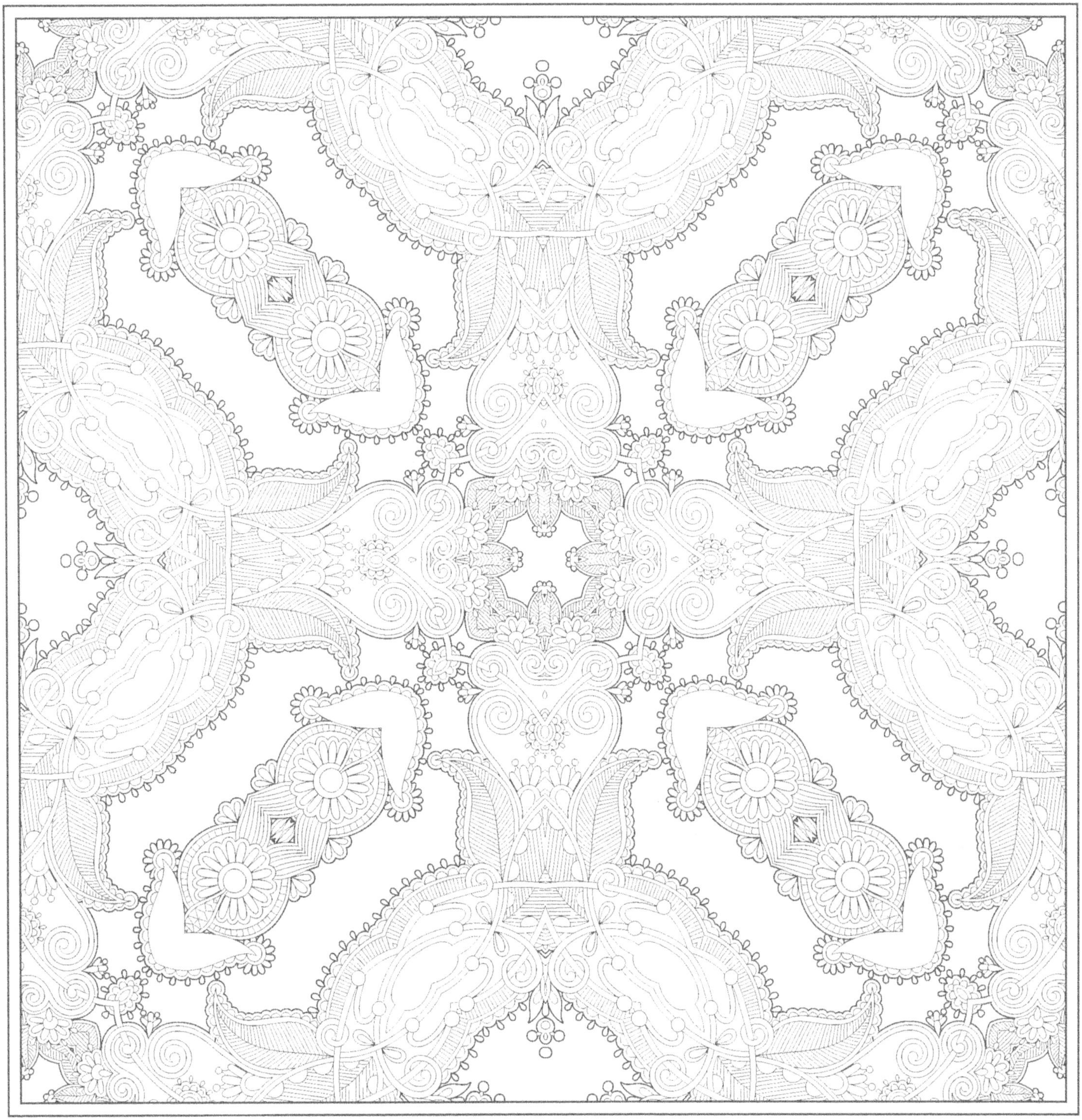

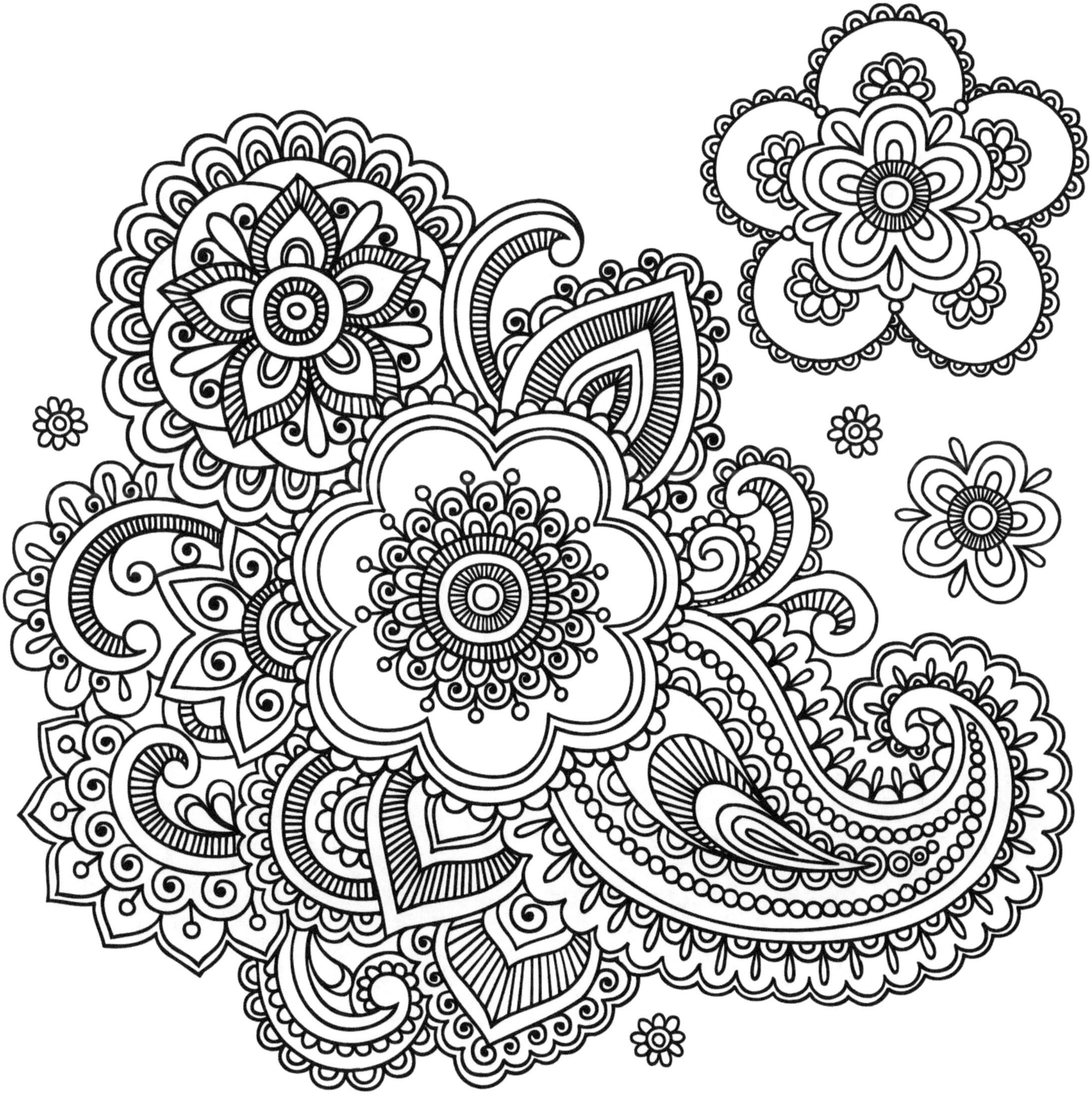

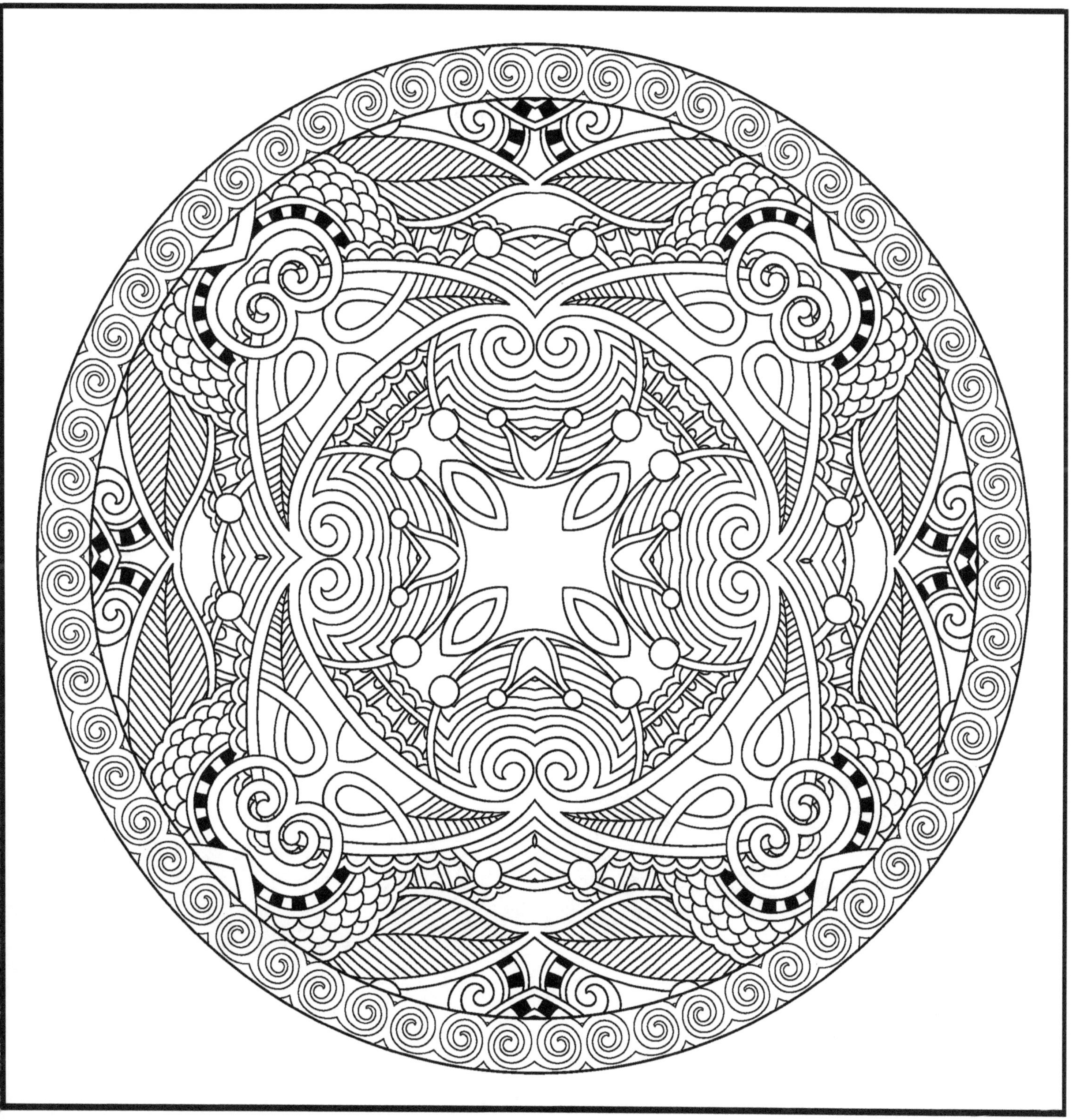

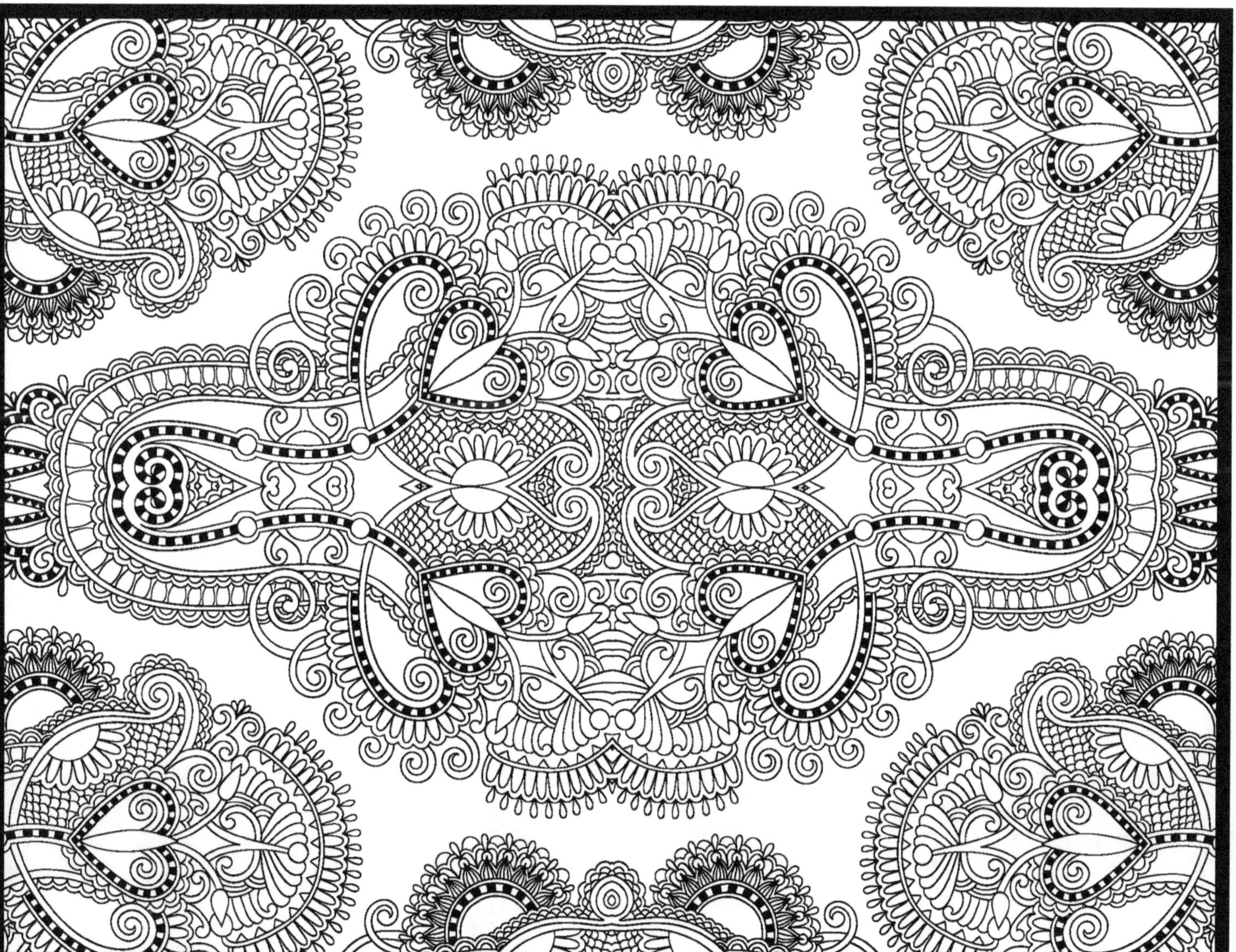

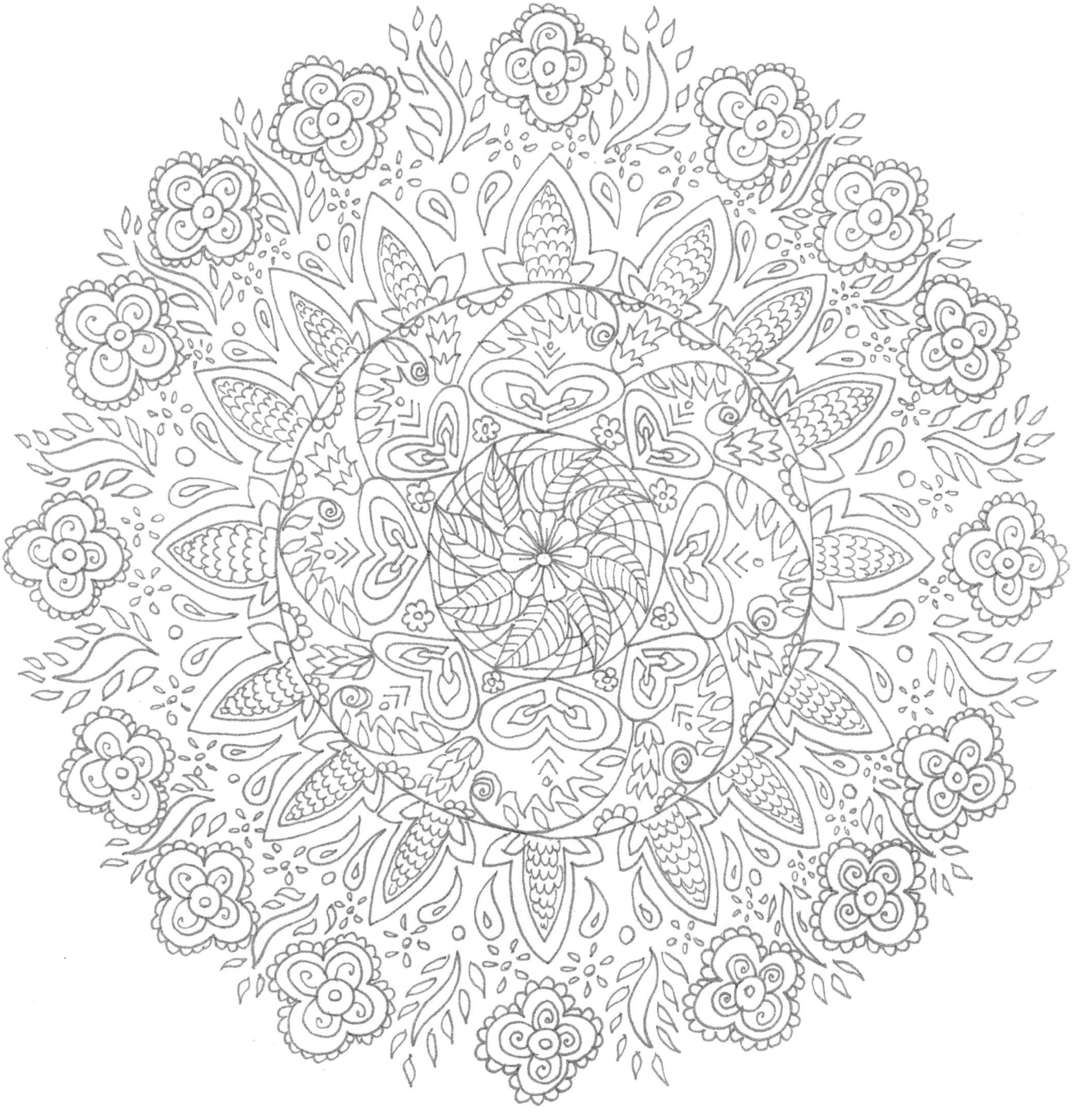

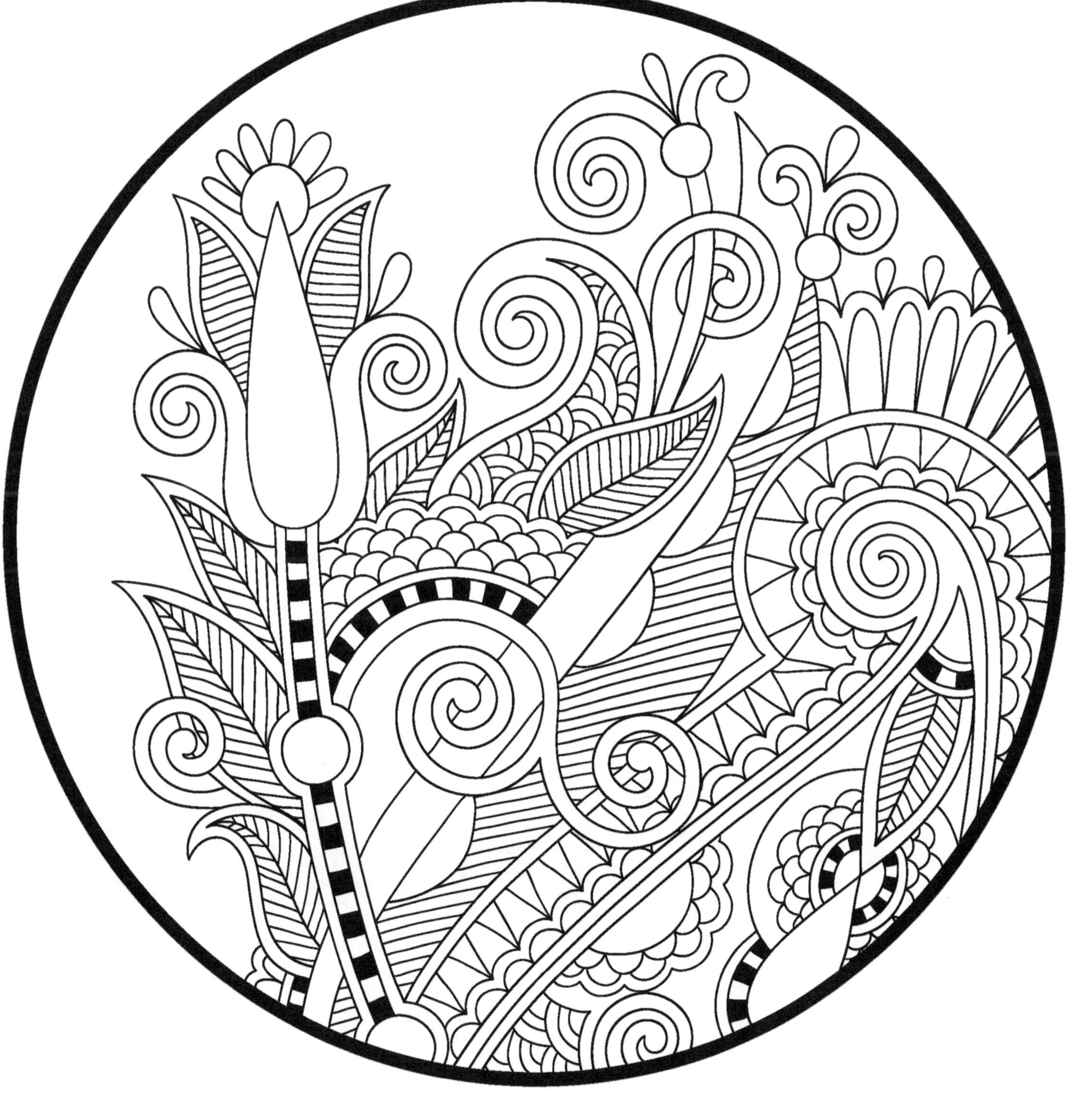

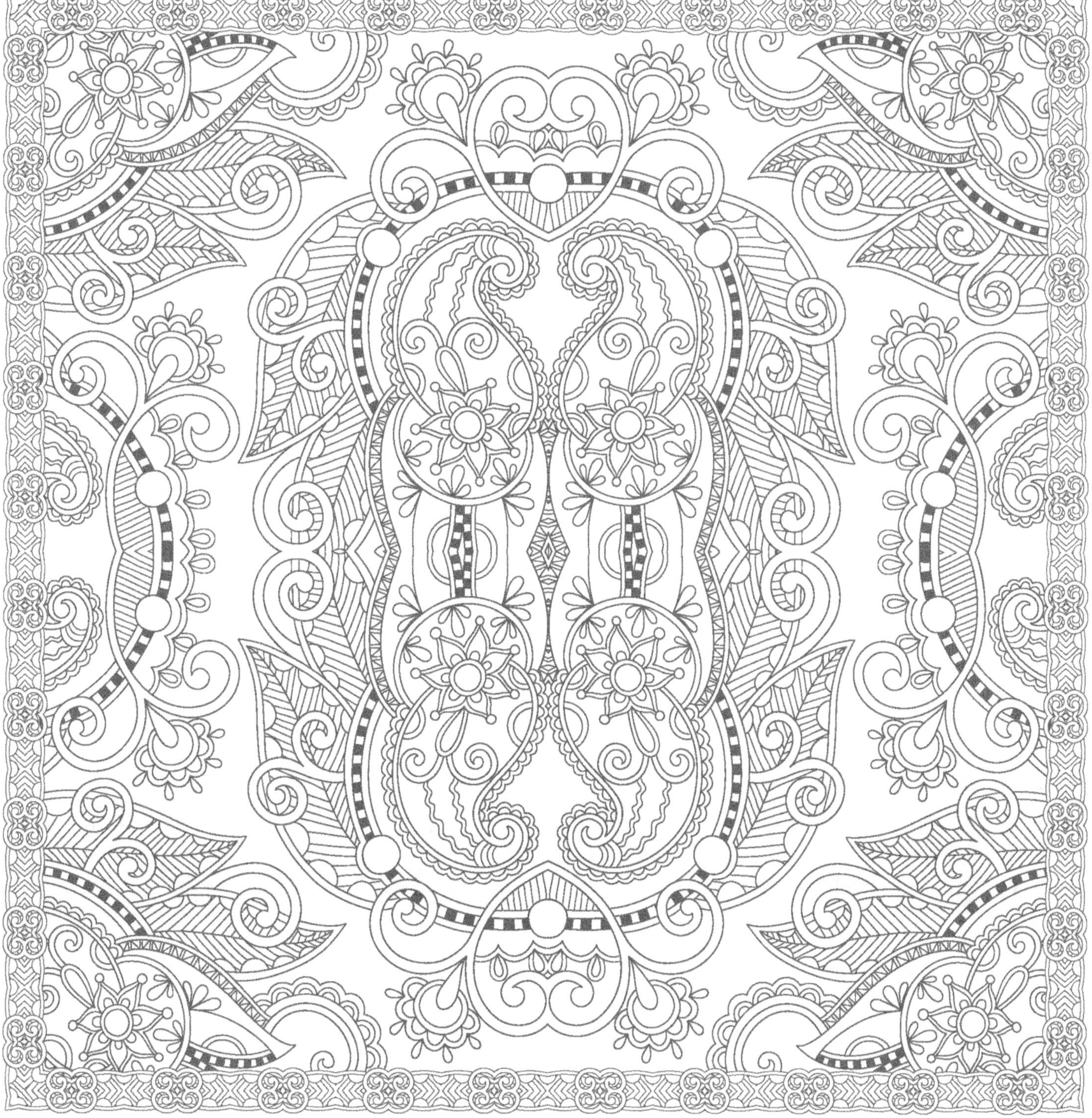

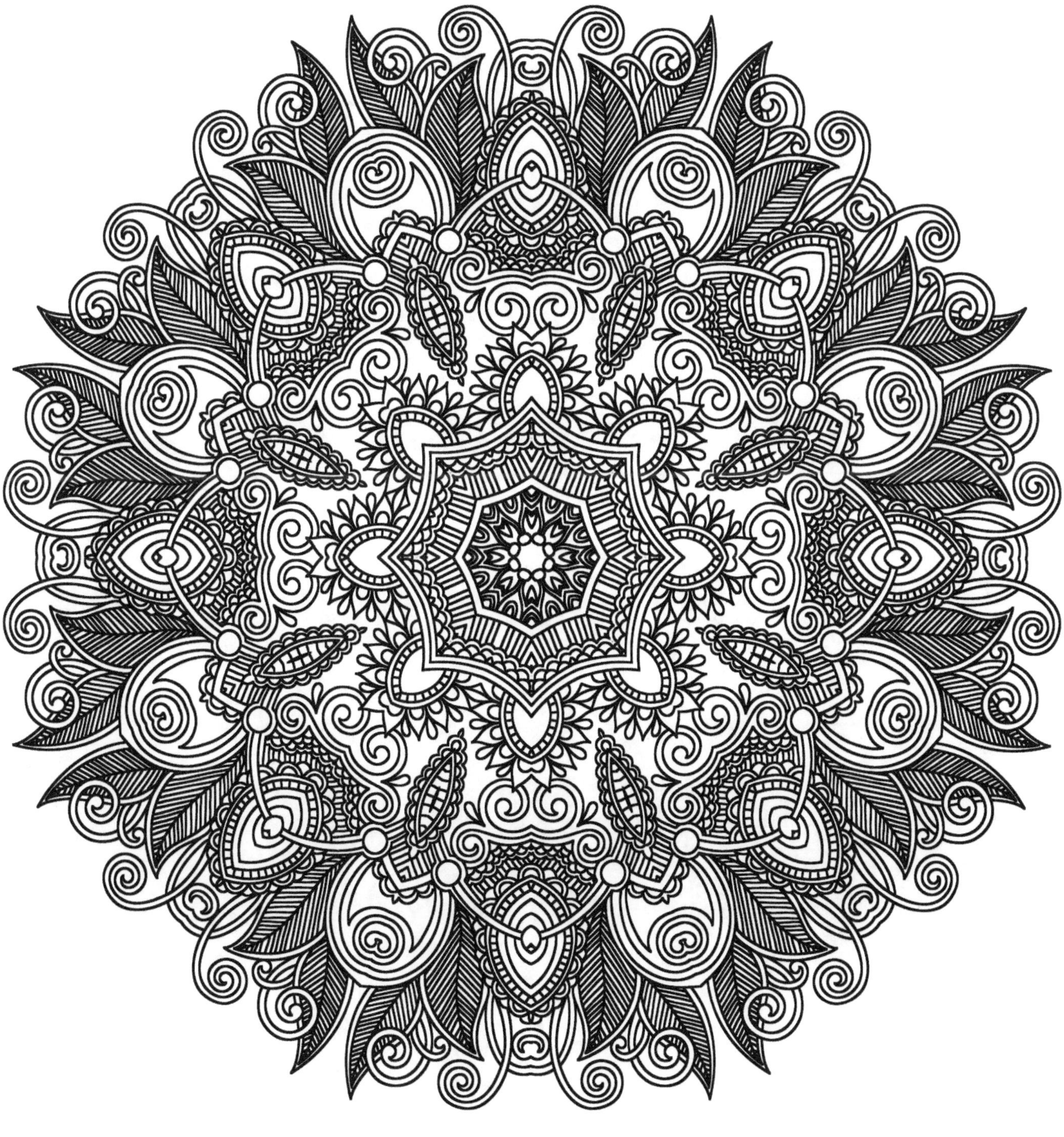

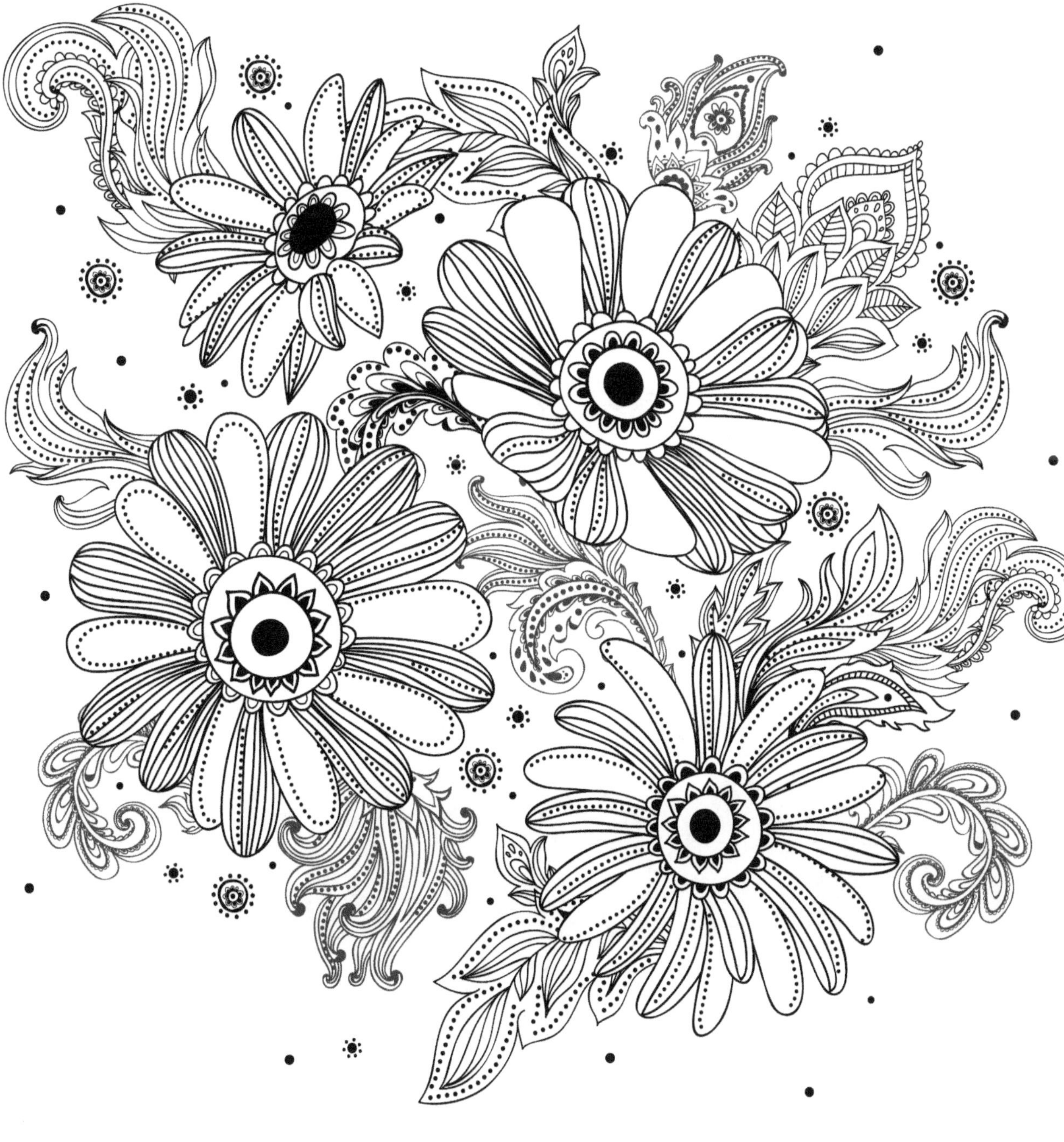

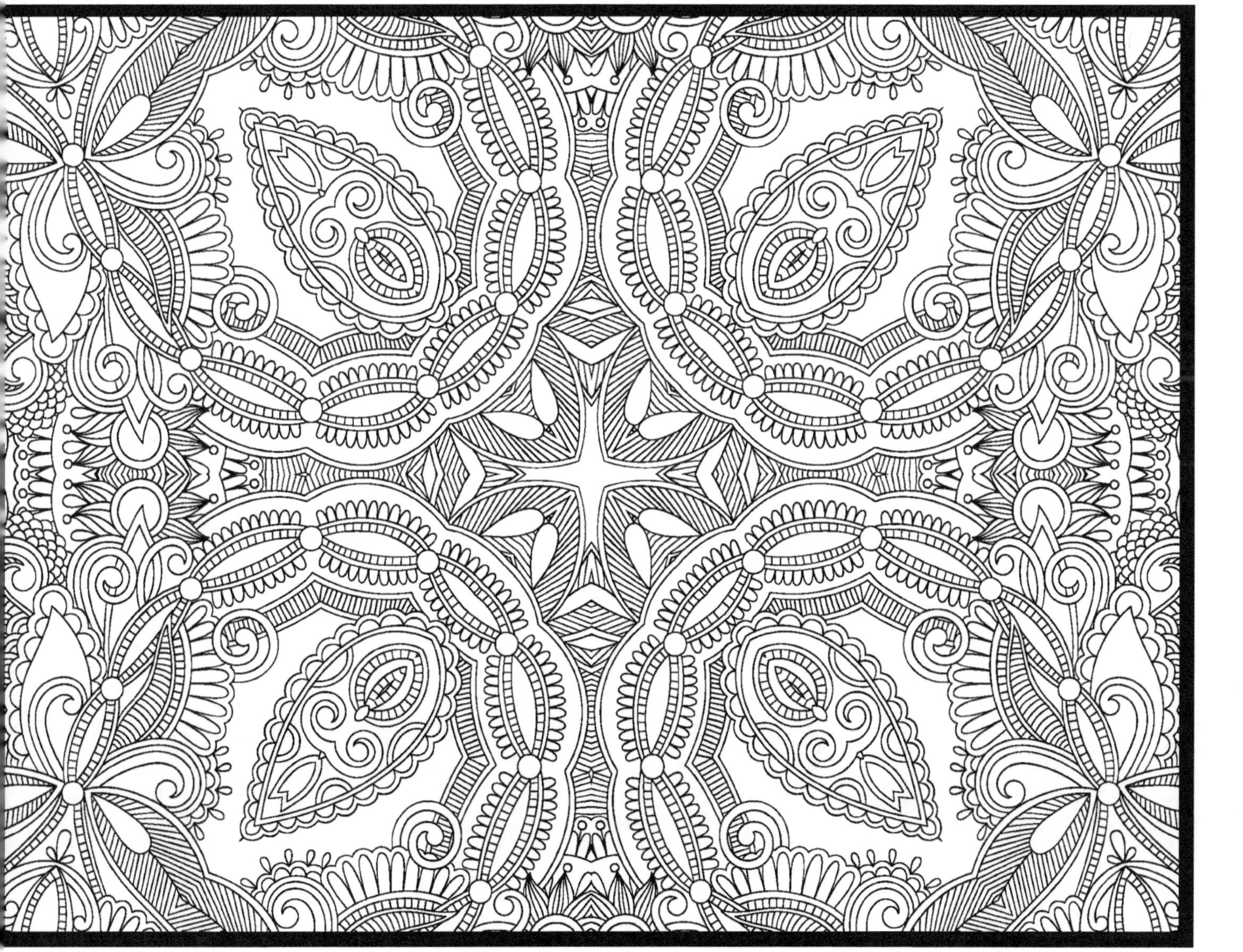

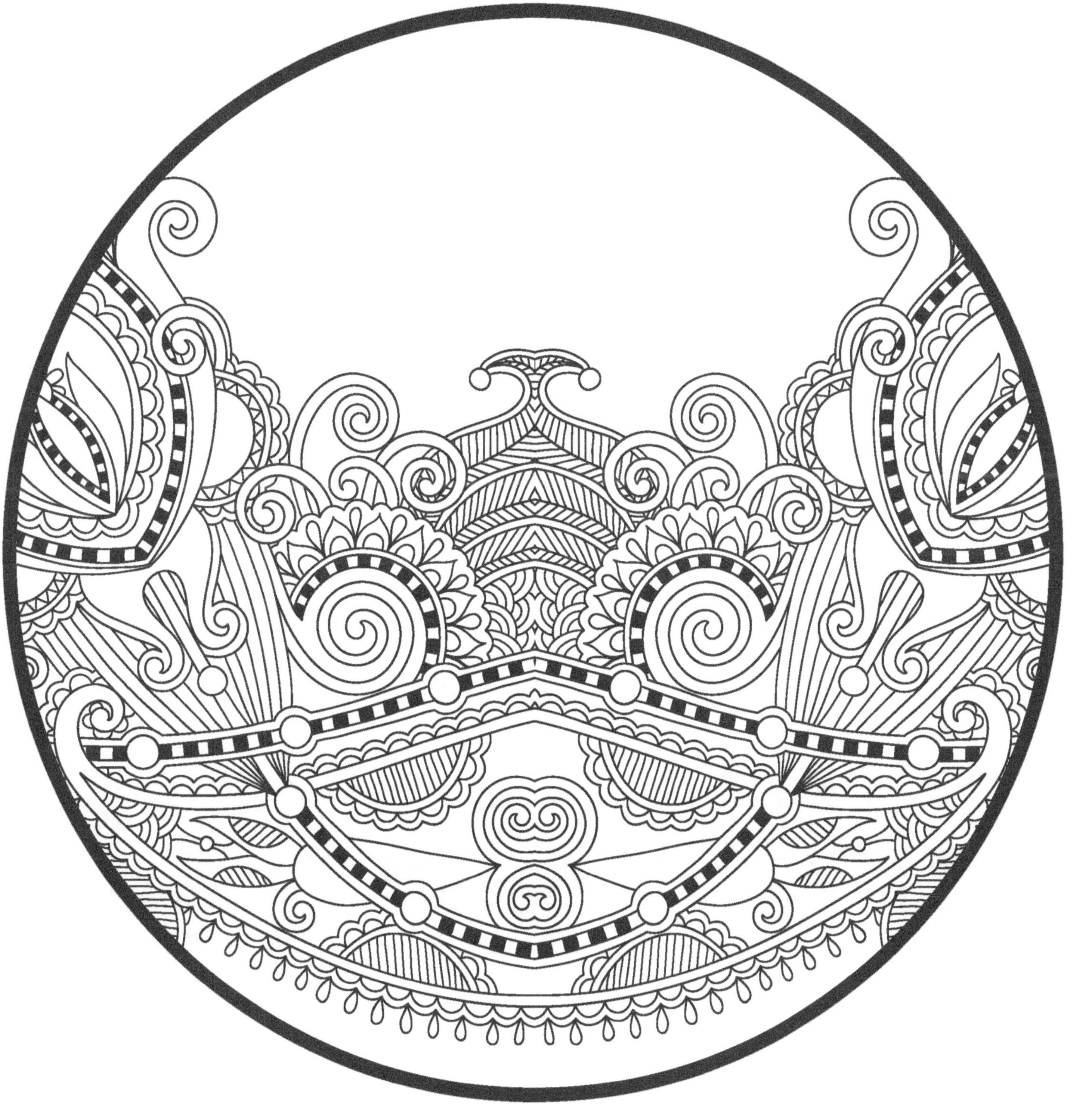

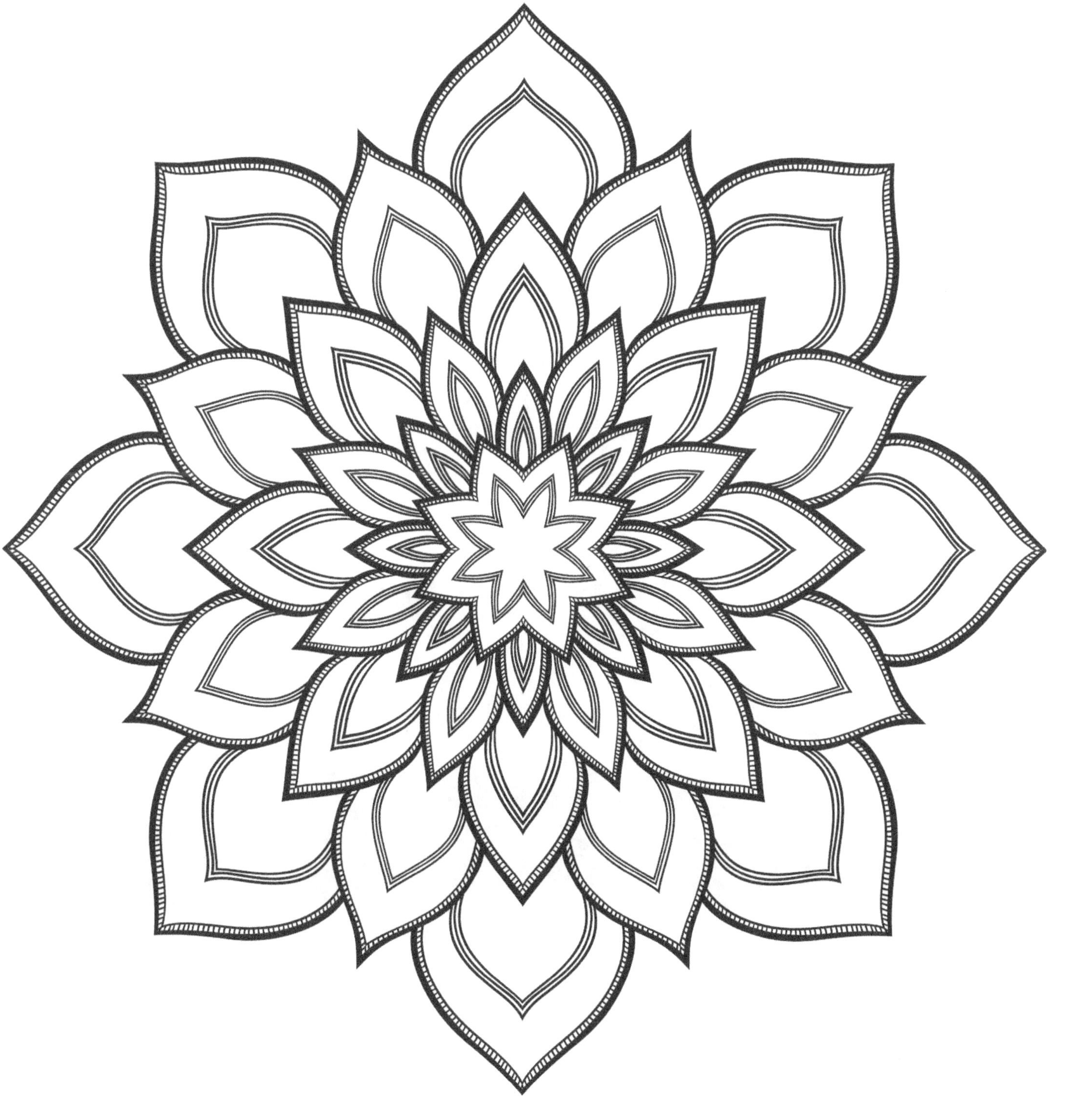

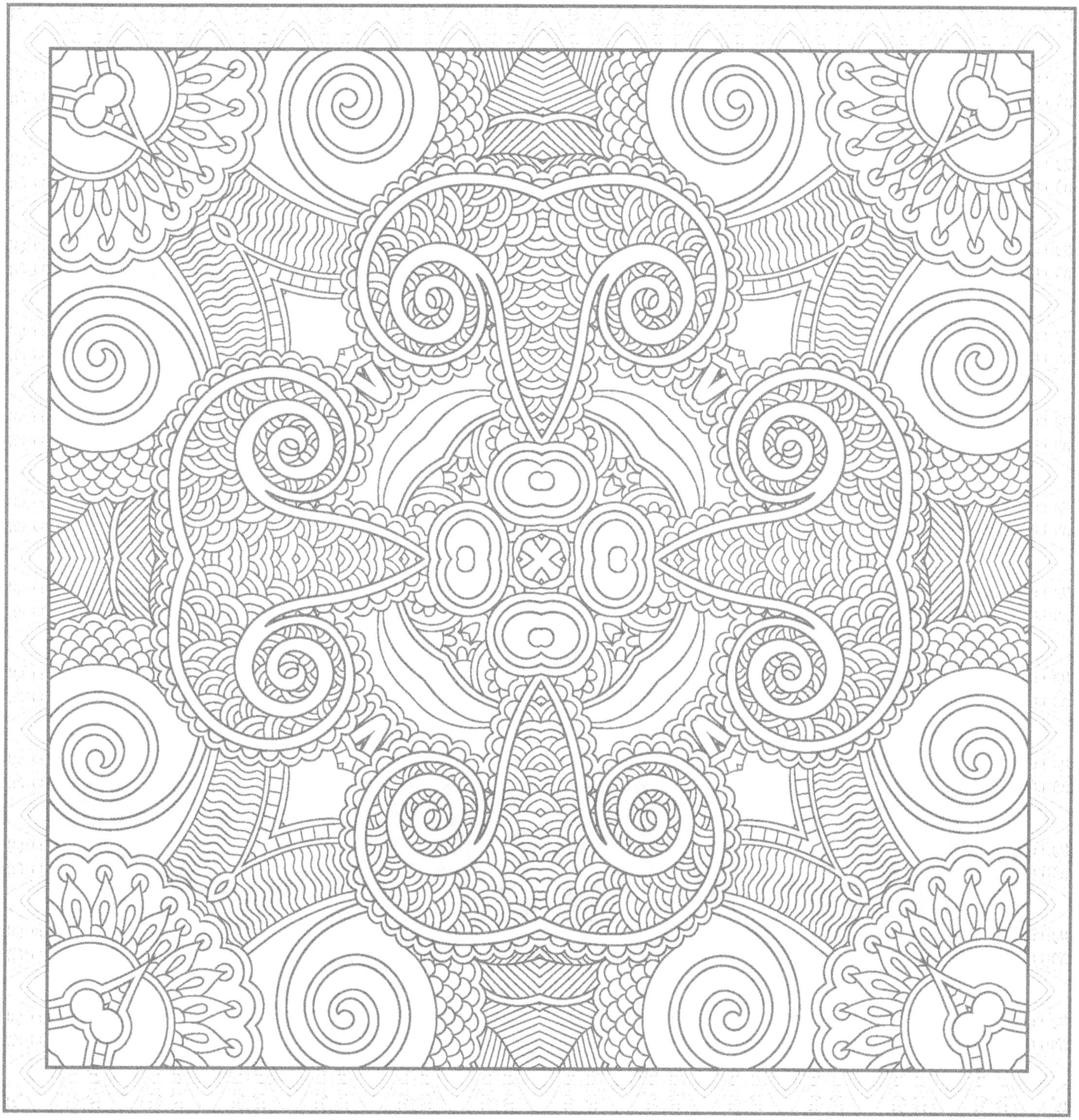

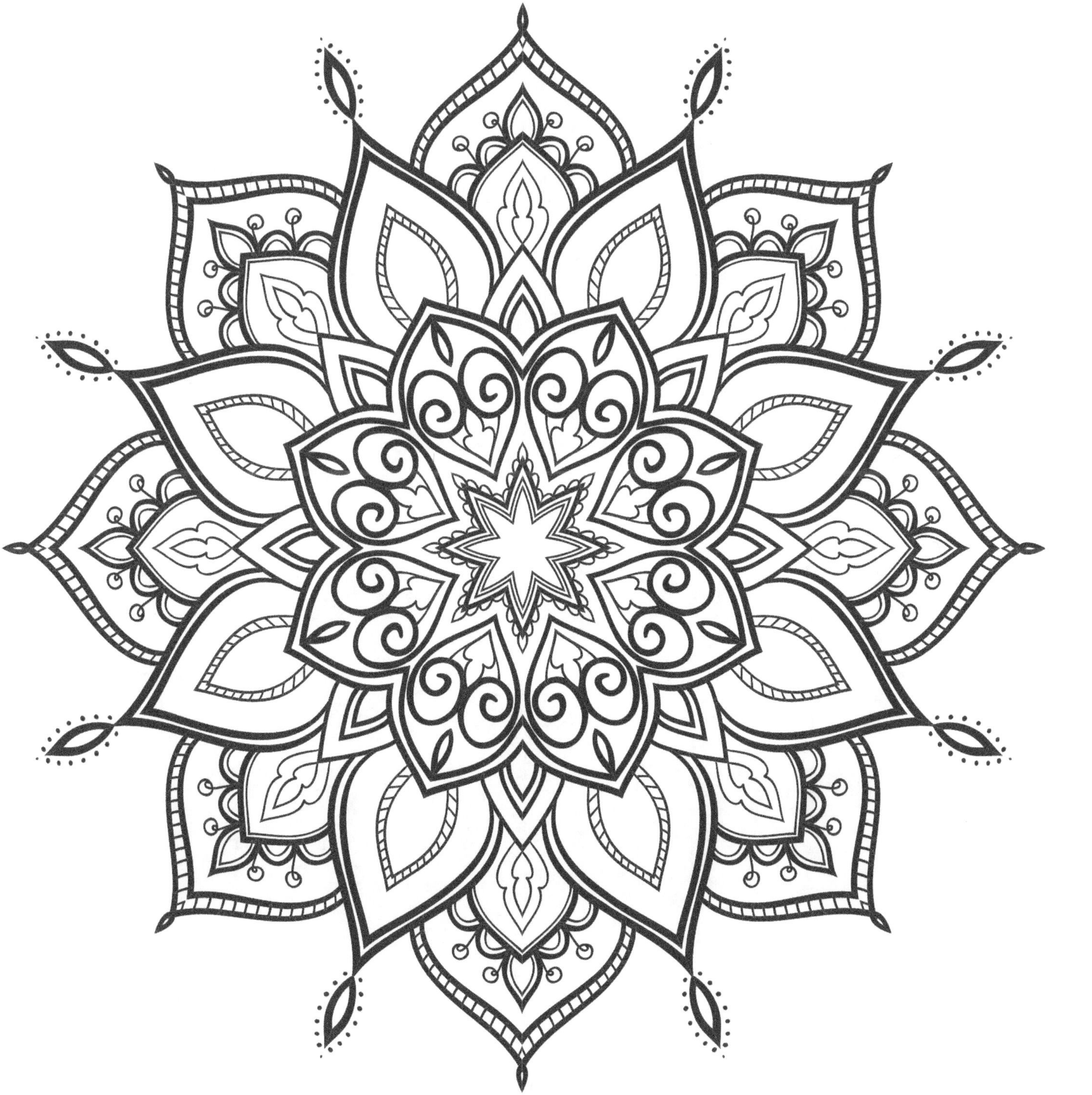

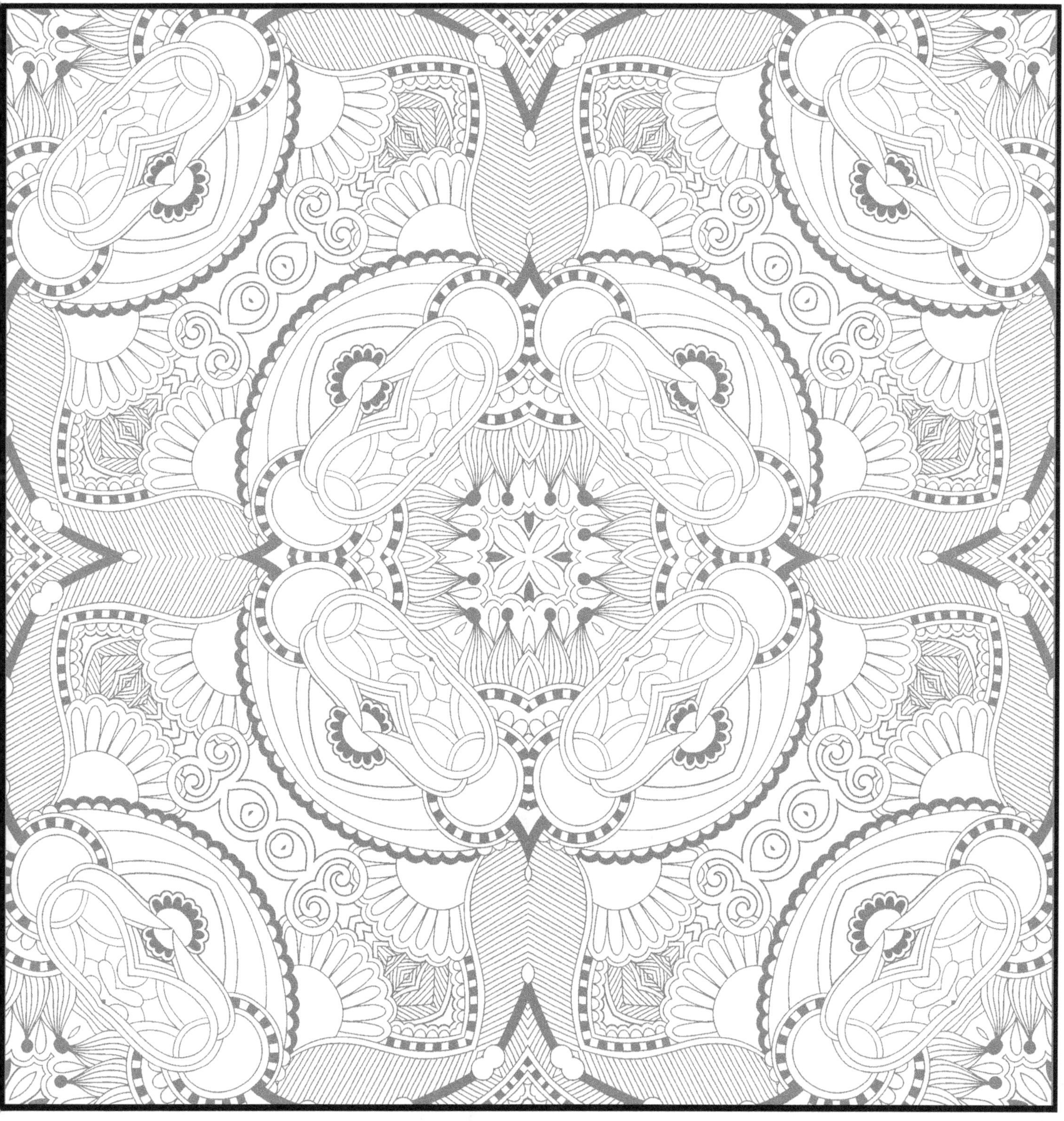

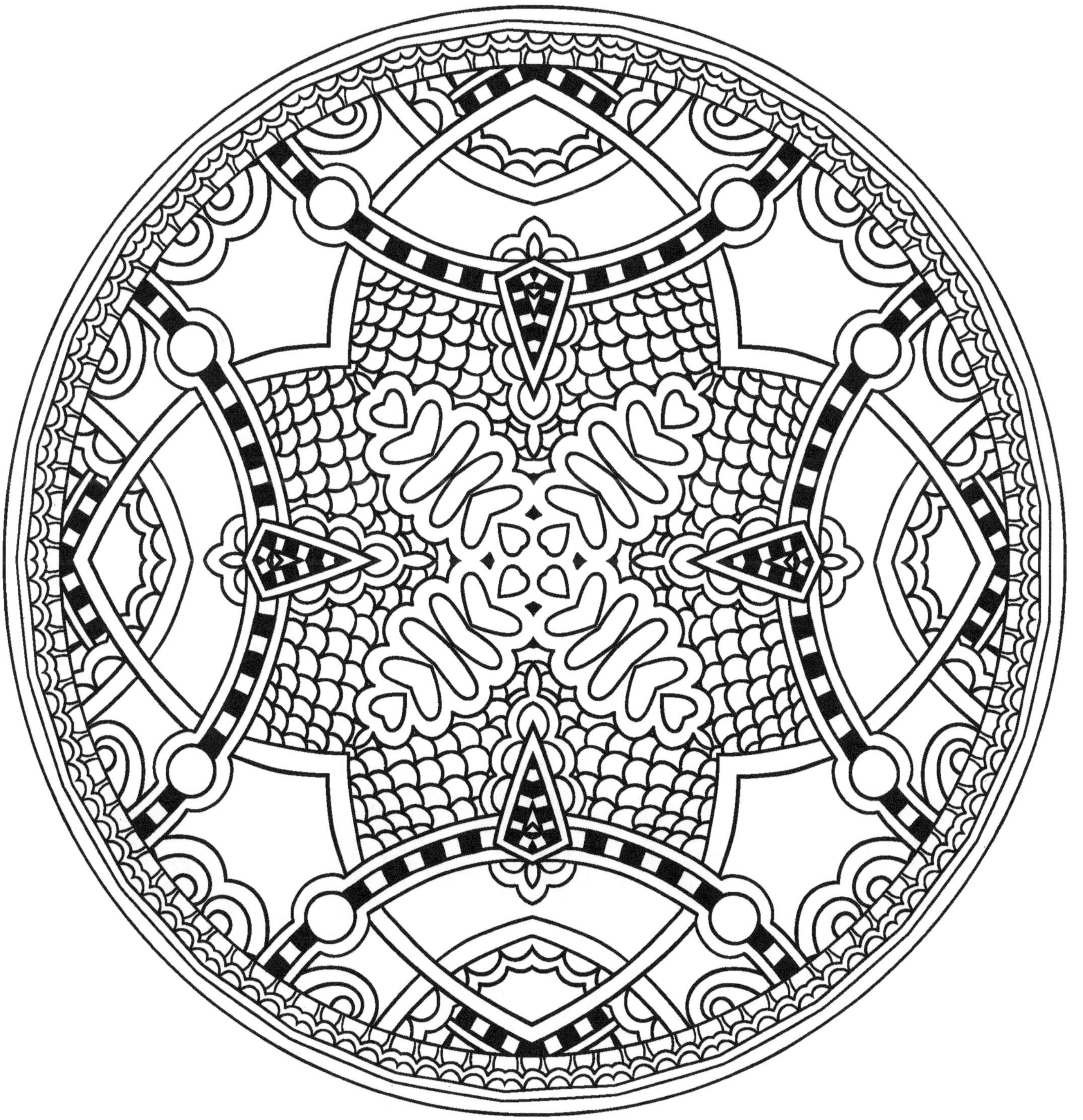

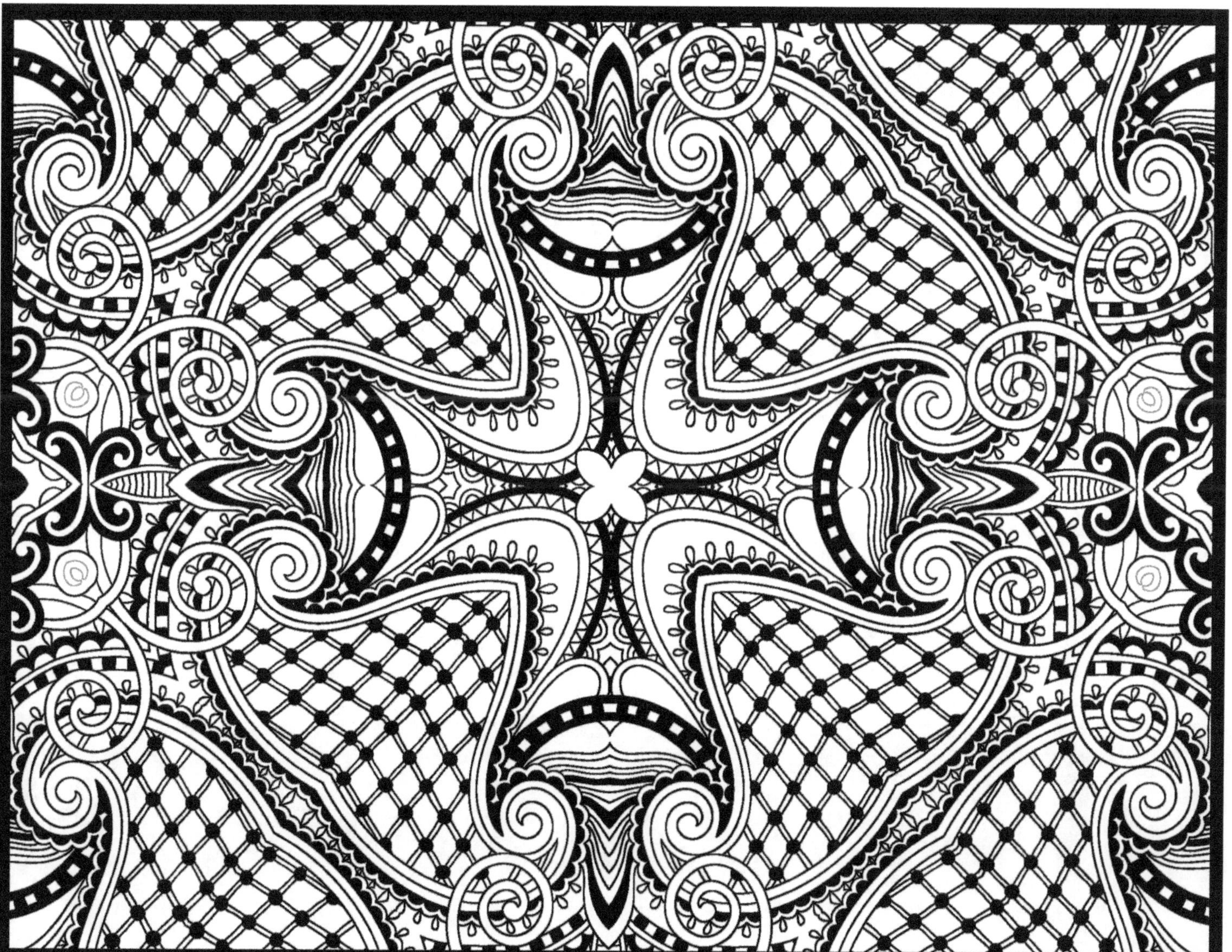

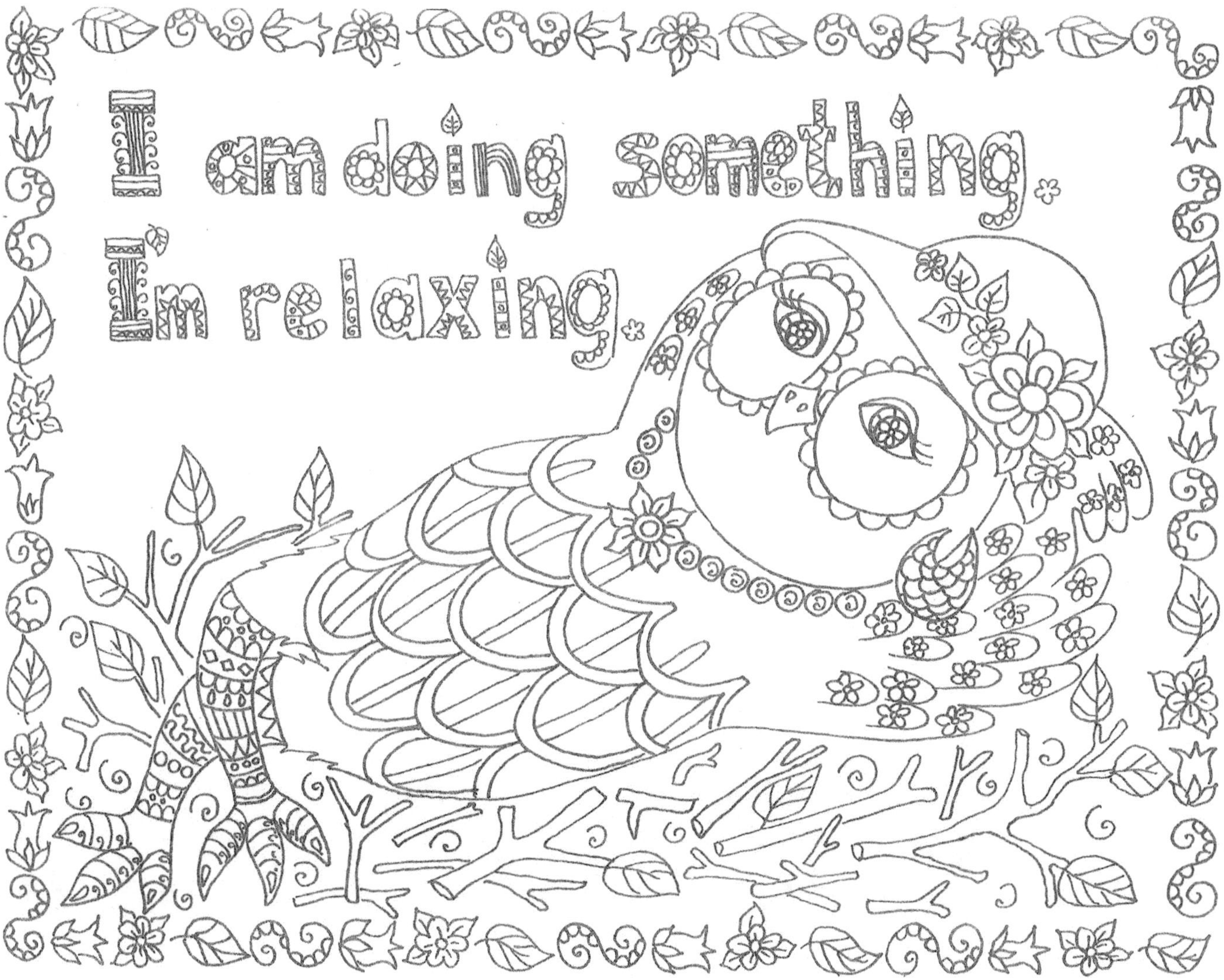
I am doing something.
I'm relaxing.

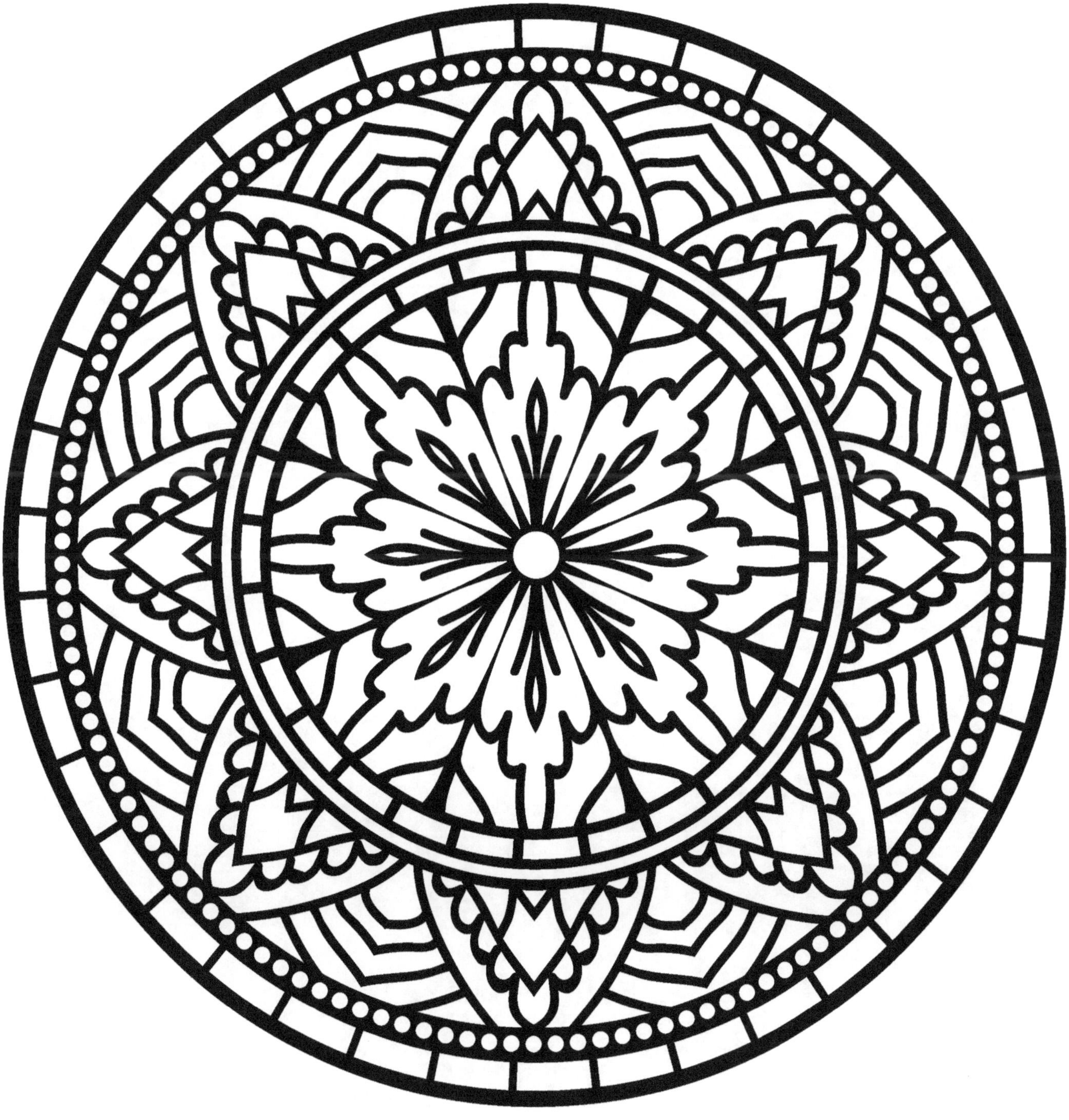

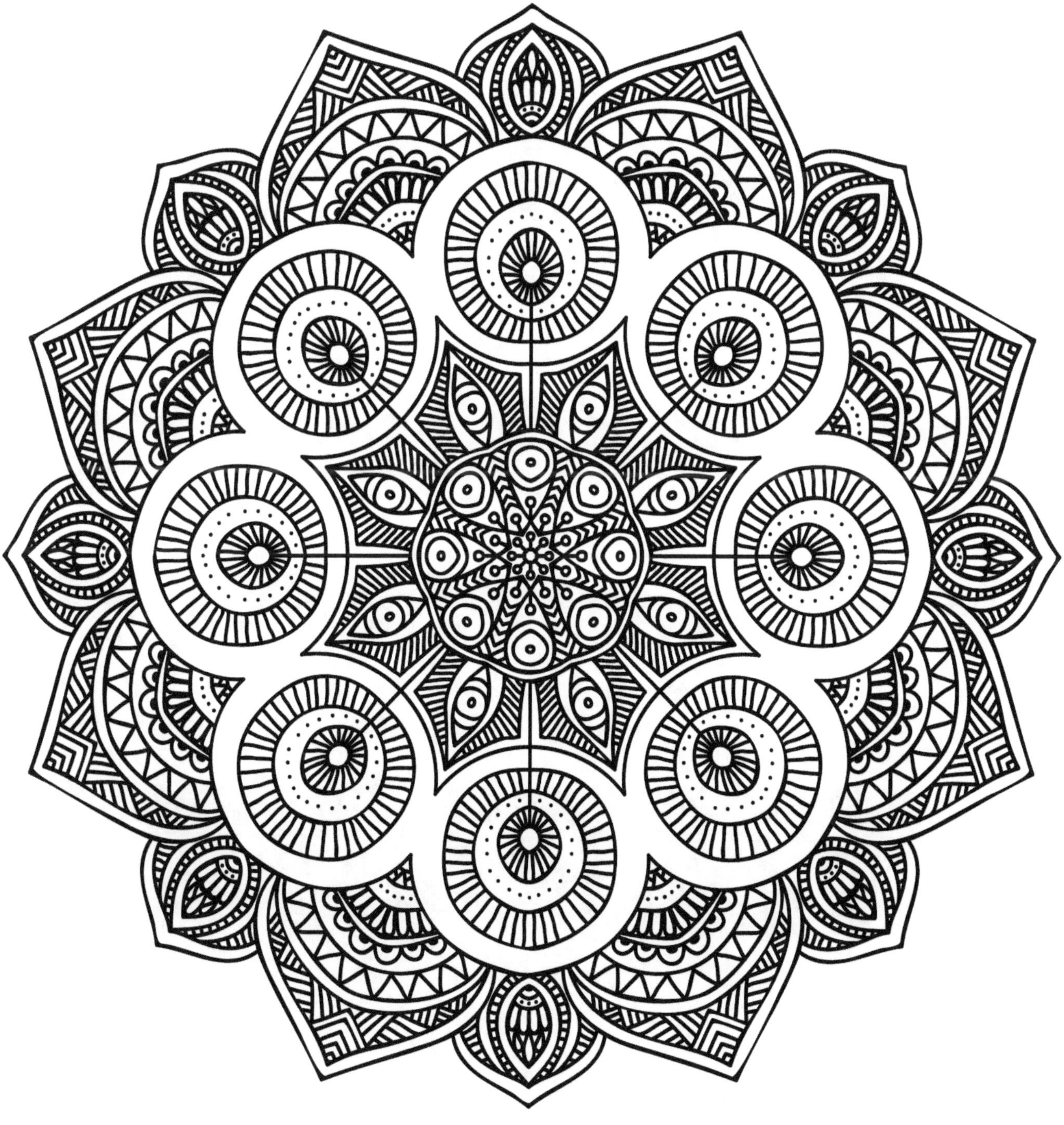

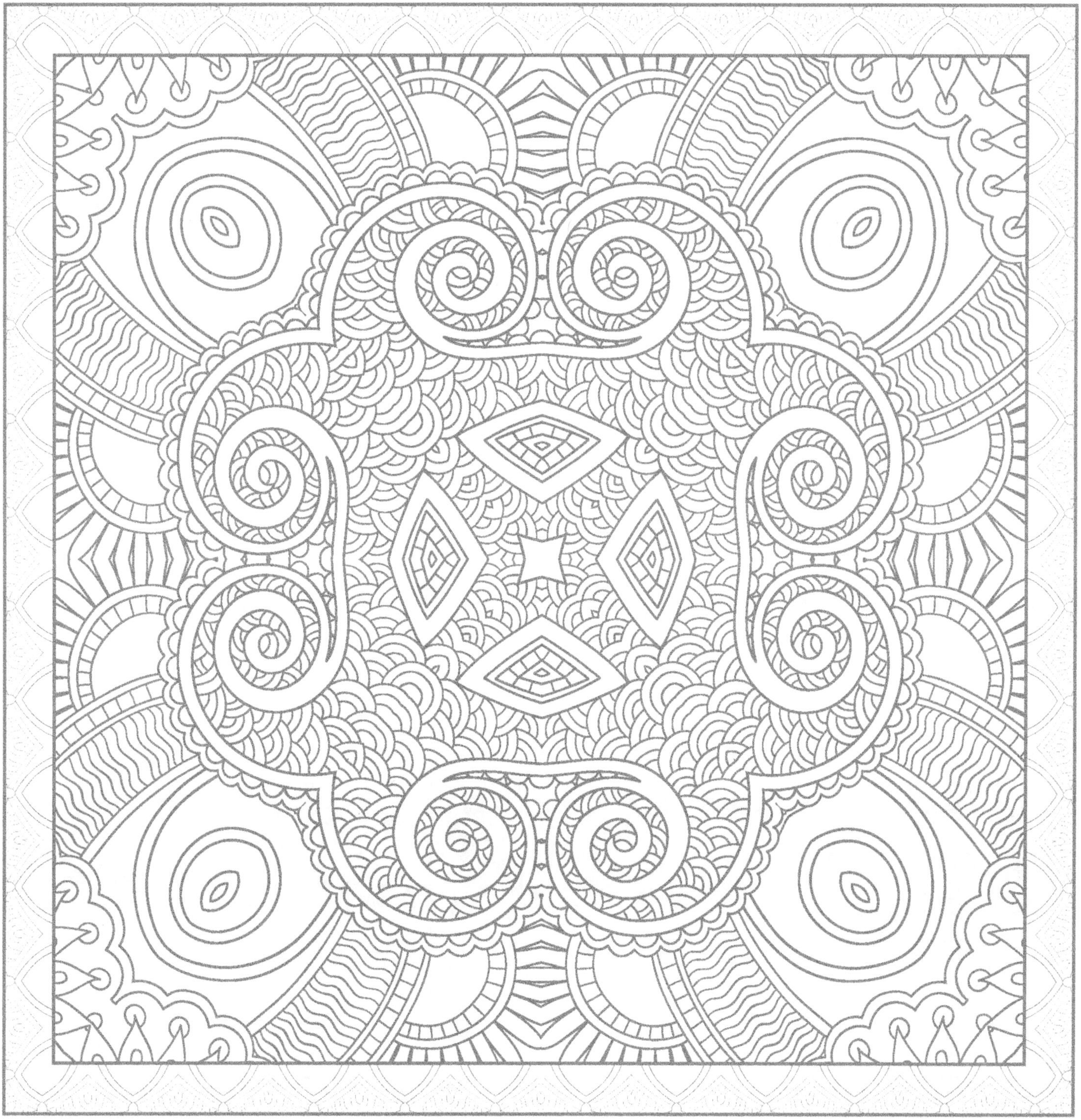

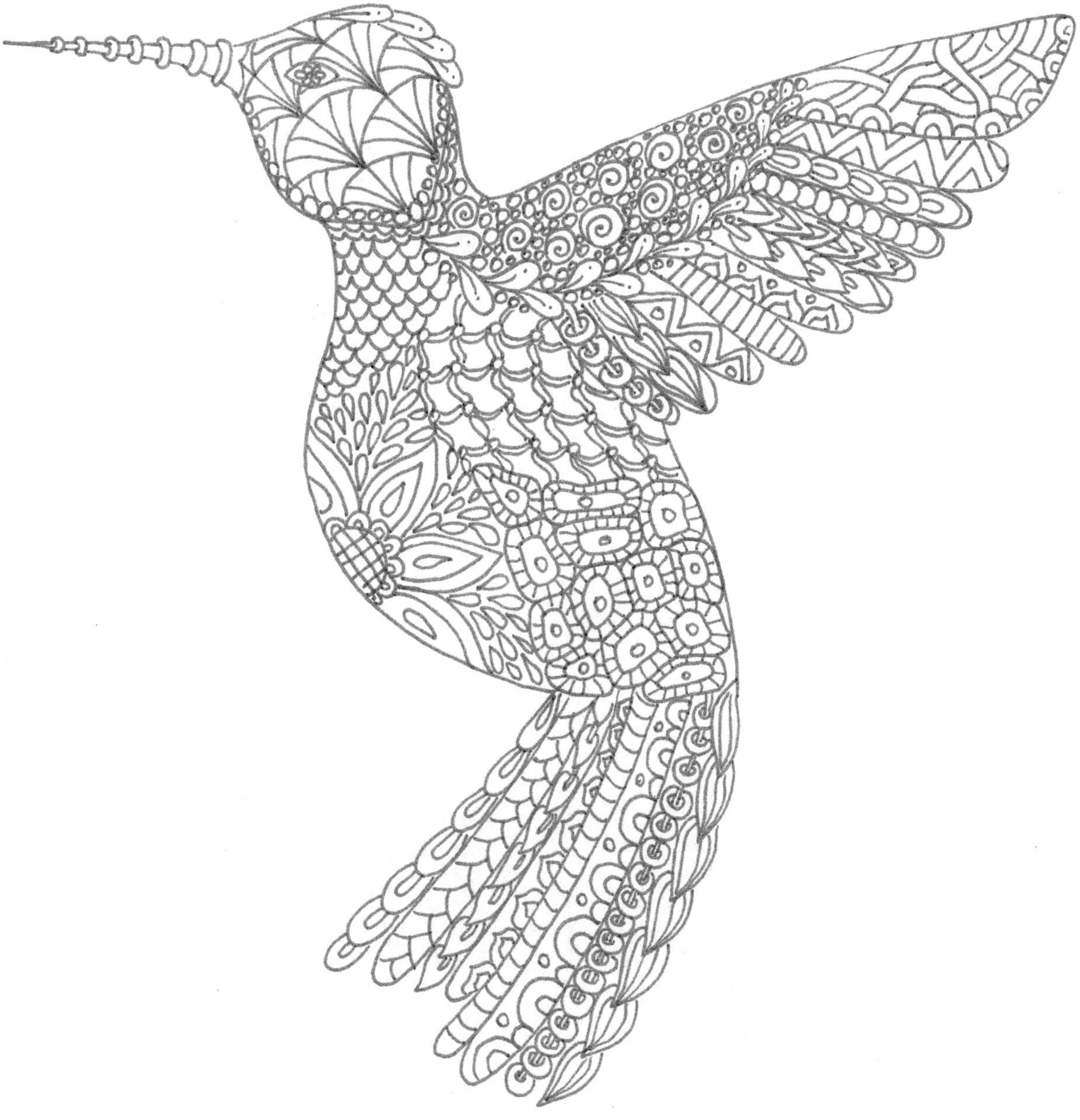

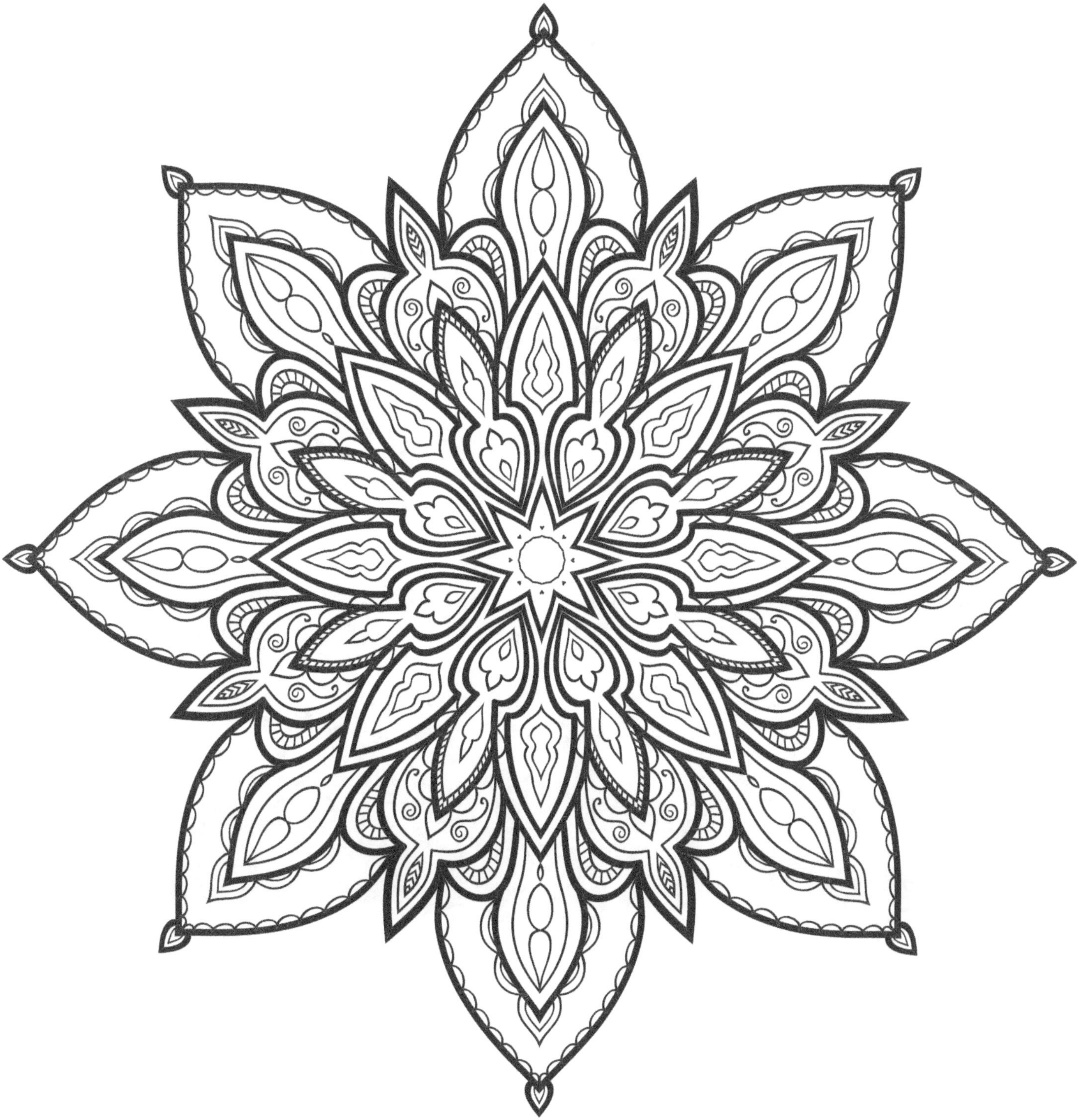

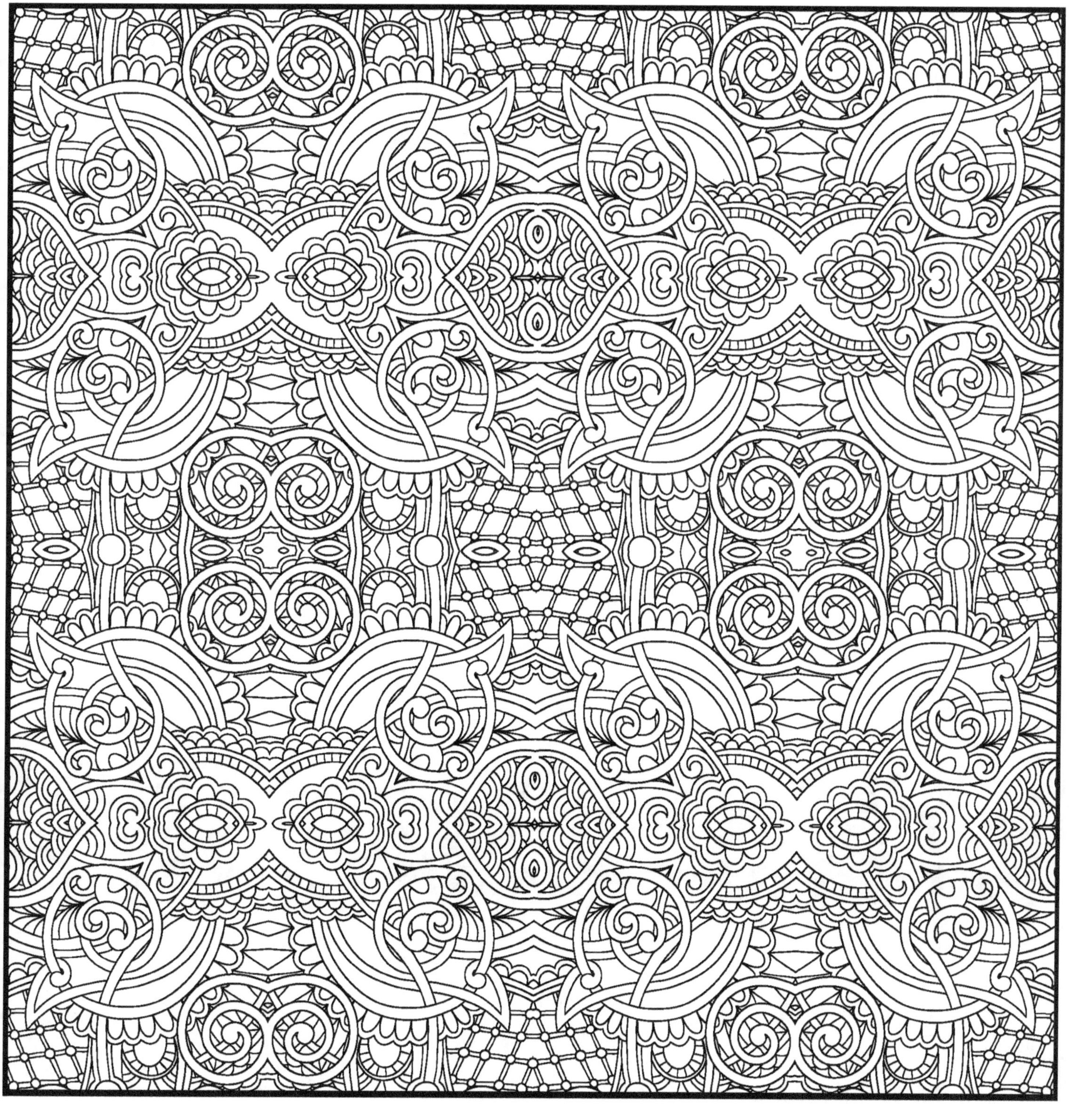

www.ingramcontent.com/pod-product-compliance
Lightning Source LLC
Chambersburg PA
CBHW081509080526
44589CB00017B/2702
* 9 7 8 1 7 7 3 8 0 0 2 4 0 *